Yale Language Series

Levantine Arabic for Non-Natives

A Proficiency-Oriented Approach

STUDENT BOOK

Lutfi Hussein

Yale University Press
New Haven and London

Copyright ©1993 by Yale University. All rights reserved.
This book may not be reproduced, in whole or in part, including illustrations, in any form (beyond that copying permitted by Sections 107 and 108 of the U. S. Copyright Law and except by reviewers for the public press), without written permission from the publishers.
Printed in the United States of America.

Library of Congress Cataloging-in-Publication Data
Hussein, Lutfi, 1955-
Levantine Arabic for non-natives: a proficiency-oriented approach: student book / Lutfi Hussein
p. cm. (Yale Language Series)
ISBN : 978-0-300-05634-1
1. Arabic language—Dialects—Syria—Texts. 2. Arabic language—Dialects—Lebanon—Texts. 3. Arabic language—Conversation and phrase books—English. 4. Arabic language—Textbooks for foreign speakers—English. I. Title
PJ6818.H87 1993
492' .77—dc20 93-15797
CIP

The Library of Congress has catalogued the Teacher's Manual as 93-15797.

A catalogue record for this book is available from the British Library.

The paper in this book meets the guidelines for permanence and durability of the Committee on Production Guidelines for Book Longevity of the Council on Library Resources.

Contents

To the Student

Part II assumes that you have studied Part I and listened to the tapes that go with it. This textbook consists of ten units and two appendices. Each unit is accompanied by an audio tape. The tapes are essential for this course. You should listen to them as often as necessary. Each tape is divided into five parts: the main text, the vocabulary list that follows, a set of statements each followed by a question, a set of conversations each followed by a question, and finally a homework. You should start listening to the first two parts as soon as you are introduced to the unit. The last three parts can be done when the whole unit has been introduced and studied thoroughly. If by then you find yourself unable to do the exercises in these three parts, review the related unit as thoroughly as you can before you restart doing them. The two appendices are meant as references and are provided for your convenience. Appendix A lists the common verbal patterns covered in Parts I and II, and Appendix B lists all the vocabulary introduced in the two parts.

The Writing System

One of the most agonizing decisions in writing this textbook was the choice of a writing system that is (1) satisfactory to the students and the instructor, and (2) capable of representing all the sounds found in Levantine Arabic with minimal degree of confusion and complexity. Obviously, the choices available were either Arabic script as it is used for Standard Arabic or an altered form of it, or a romanized writing form. After studying the advantages and disadvantages of each it was decided that a romanized writing system would be the lesser of the two evils. Some of the advantages of using a romanized writing system are:

1. It represents all the sounds found in Levantine Arabic. By contrast, Arabic script lacks the orthographical symbols for the sound /ee/ as in words like /xeer/ "good," /oo/ as in words like /yoom/ "a day," and /e/ as in words like /hiyye/ "she."

2. It solves the problem of multiple representation that would have arisen had Arabic script been chosen. For example, the Standard Arabic letter /ث/ has been replaced in this dialect by /t/ in words such as /θaani/, /θaaliθ/, and /s/ in words such as /maθalan/, /θaabit/, and it remains in words such as /?amθaal/. In this case, /θ/, had Arabic script been used, would have been realized as standing for three different, and indeed phonemically distinct, sounds in this variety of Arabic. Similar problems arise when we analyze the status of the glottal stop (i.e., hamza), which is represented as /y/ in words such as /daa?ira/, /æ:/ in words such as /ra?s/, /u:/ in words such as /ru?u:s/, and remains hamza in words such as /ra?i:s/. Other sounds that exhibit similar problems are /ق/, /ذ/, /ظ/, and /ض/.

3. The use of a romanized form saves the principle of authenticity intact. This variety of Arabic, like all vernacular varieties, is used for oral communication only. It lacks any Arabic orthographical representation, though in recent years some novelists have started to introduce some of it in their writings. This use (i.e., in novels) is actually minimal and the Arabic script used is not standardized. It often slows down the reader and occasionally aggravates him. The reader tends to rely on his

knowledge of the dialect to decipher the written text instead of relying on the accuracy of the writing symbols used.

4. Using a romanized writing system is not a new phenomenon in teaching colloquial Arabic. Most of the textbooks used in teaching the colloquial varieties of Arabic have been written in romanized writing systems. More important, the reference books and dictionaries are also written in romanized alphabet.[1] Breaking from such a tradition would leave the students stranded after they complete the course covered in this book had Arabic script been used. The use of a romanized form would place them in the mainstream and equip them with the knowledge (i.e., writing system) needed to pursue learning the variety on their own if they decide to do so.

These are some of the reasons for choosing a romanized alphabet over Arabic script. The following is a list of the writing symbols used in this textbook:

A. Vowels

/i/ Short vowel similar to /i/ in "hit" represented in Standard Arabic (SA henceforth) by *kasra* (____ِ).

/ii/ Long /i/ similar to the vowel in "meet" and written in SA as ي

/a/ Short vowel similar to /a/ in "at" and written in SA as *fatha* (____َ).

/aa/ Long /a/ similar to /a/ in "mat" and written in SA as أ

/u/ Short vowel similar to /u/ in "put" and written in Arabic as *damma* (____ُ).

/uu/ Long /u/ similar to /oo/ in "food" and written in SA as و

/e/ Short vowel similar to /e/ in "met" and does not have any representation in SA.

/ee/ Long /e/ similar to /a/ in "make" and does not have any representation in SA.

/oo/ Long /o/ and similar to /o/ in "go" and does not have any representation in SA.

B. Consonants

Most of the symbols used in this textbook are those of the International Phonetic Alphabet (IPA). Some of the symbols used in this system that might be confusing are:

/H/ stands for voiceless pharyngeal fricative, written in SA as ح

/?/ stands for glottal stop (i.e., hamza) ء

---

[1]The two major references available for foreign students learning Levantine Arabic are A Dictionary of Syrian Arabic: English-Arabic by Stowasser and Ani and Reference Grammar of Syrian Arabic by Cowell. Both are written in a romanized form.

/x/ stands for the Arabic sound خ

/γ/ stands for the Arabic sound غ

/š/ stands for the Arabic sound ش

Superscripted /^{c}/ stands for voiced pharyngeal fricative, written in SA as ع
Double consonants are used to express gemination.
Capital letters stand for emphatic sounds and small letters stand for plain ones.

It is rather tempting for students in such a course to create their own systems of writing. It has actually happened several times in the past. Such a process tends to confuse the instructor who has to grade students' homework, some of the written exercises, and occasionally some tests. It also often leads to a breakdown of communication with other students when it comes to reading each other's notes. To eliminate such problems and standardize everybody's writing, it is important that you (students and instructors) learn this system and adhere to it throughout the whole course.

riHla ^{c}ala madiinat New York

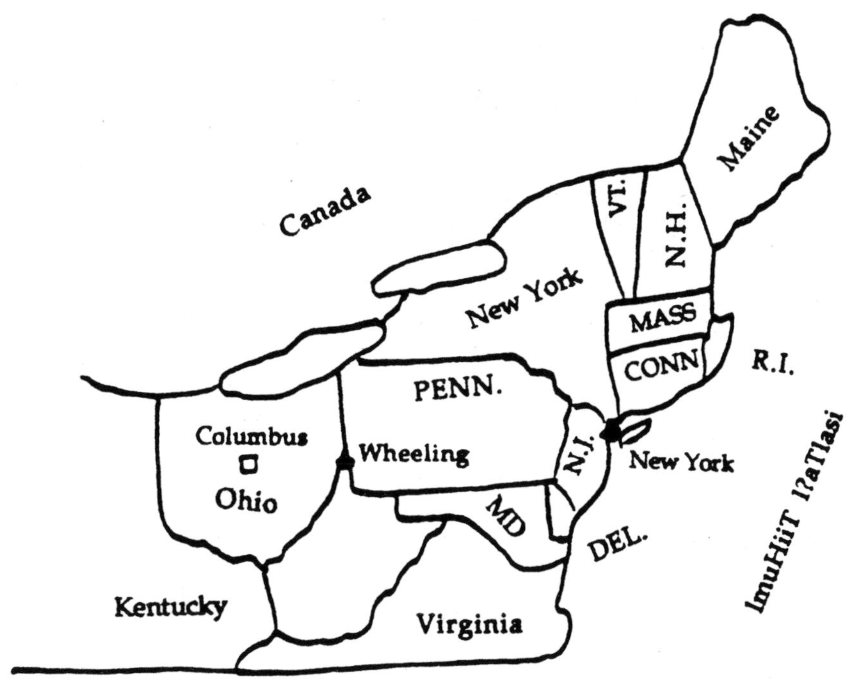

fi ^{c}uTlit faSil rrabii^{c} raaH Bruce wSadii?tu Sandy ^{c}ala madiinat New York. kaanat muddit rriHla xamis ?ayyaam. ?a^{c}adu fi New York talat ?ayyaam wyomeen ^{c}ala TTarii?. Tili^{c} Bruce wSandy ssee^{c}a sab^{c}a SSubH yoom ljum^{c}a min Columbus fi sayyaarit Toyota zγiira. kaanat ššams Taal^{c}a wiljaww mumtaaz. saa? ssayyaara Bruce min Columbus la Wheeling fi West Virginia. hunaak wa??afu lamuddat nuSS see^{c}a ta?riiban. ?akalu wajbit lifTuur witrayyaHu šwayy. ba^{c}deen Sandy badat tsuu?. kaanat TTarii? Tawiila wmut^{c}iba. Dallu ysuu?u Hatta lmaγrib. marraat saa? Bruce wmarraat saa?at Sandy. wiSlu madiinat New York ssee^{c}a tis^{c}a lmaγrib. li?anhum Tullaab wma^{c}hummiš fluus ktiira, ?a^{c}adu ?aktar min see^{c}a ydawru ^{c}ala ?uteel rxiiS. fi l?axiir nizlu fi ?uteel il-YMCA fi Manhattan. lamma wiSlu l?uteel kaanu joo^{c}aaniin wta^{c}baaniin. ?akalu wnaamu ^{c}ala Tuul. taani yoom ?aamu ssee^{c}a ^{c}ašara SSubH wbadu yitjawwalu fi šawaari^{c} Manhattan. šaafu ?ašyaa? (?ašaaya) ktiira mitil naaTiHaat ssaHaab wmabna l?umam lmutaHida wba^{c}D lmaHallaat ttijaariyya. tγaddu hadaak lyoom fi maT^{c}am zγiir fi šaari^{c} 5th. wrij^{c}u lmaγrib ^{c}ala l?uteel. ssee^{c}a tamaanya raaHu ^{c}ala sinama ?ariiba wHaDaru film fukaahi. taalit yoom

?aamu ssee^{c}a tis^{c}a wbadu jawla taanya fi Manhattan. šaafu fi hadaak lyoom timsaal lHuriyya, wjaziirat Ellis, wTil^{c}u bilma^{c}diyya ^{c}ala Staten Island. lmaγrib raaHu ^{c}ala baar wširbu biira wšwayyit kuHuul. rij^{c}u ^{c}ala l?uteel ssee^{c}a ^{c}ašara lmaγrib wnaamu.

raabi^{c} yoom Til^{c}u bissayyaara wraaHu ^{c}ala Long Island. raaHu ^{c}ala šaTT lbaHar. sabaHu witšammasu wli^{c}bu kurat rriiša. Dallu ^{c}ala šaTT lbaHar Hatta ssee^{c}a talaata ba^{c}id DDuhur. ba^{c}deen libsu malaabishum wraaHu yzuuru Sadii?hum Andy. Andy kaan yistanna fiihum lamma wiSlu ssee^{c}a xamsa ba^{c}d DDuhur. ra?san tγaddu w?a^{c}adu yitkallmu ^{c}an Columbus wOhio State wriHlithum ^{c}ala madiinat New York. lmaγrib tfarraju ^{c}ala lu^{c}bit kurat ssalla been Columbia wPrinceton. naamu hadiik lleela fi beet Andy wtaani yoom rij^{c}u ^{c}ala Columbus. Sandy wBruce nbasaTu ktiir fi riHlithum wrij^{c}u musta^{c}iddiin lalfaSl ljaay.

timsaal lHuriyya

mabna l?umam lmutaHida

NaTiHaat ssaHaab, Manhattan

lmufradaat

^{c}uTla	break
riHla (pl. riHlaat)	trip
mudda	period
?a^{c}ad (ba^{cc}ud)[1]	to stay, to sit down
Tarii? (pl. Turu?)	road, way
Tili^{c} (baTla^{c})	to get out, leave
ššams	the sun
Taali^{c}	rising
saa? (basuu?)	to drive
wa??af (bawa??if)	to stop
bada (babdi)	to start
mut^{c}ib	tiresome, exhausting
Dall (baDall)	to continue, to go on
li?annu	because of
dawwar (badawwir)	to look for
fi l?axiir	at last
nizil (banzil)	to stay in, to lodge in
joo^{c}aan	hungry
ta^{c}baan	tired
^{c}ala Tuul	right away
tjawwal (batjawwal)	to wander, to walk around
ši (pl. ?ašyaa?)	thing
mitil	such as
naaTiHaat ssaHaab	skyscrapers
l?umam lmutaHida	the United Nations
maHal tijaari (pl. maHallaat tijaariyya)	store
HaDar (baHDur)	to attend, to watch
jawla (pl. jawlaat)	tour
timsaal lHuriyya	Statue of Liberty
jaziira (pl. jazaa?ir)	island
ma^{c}diyya	ferry

[1] All verbs will be given in the past tense form of the third person singular as is customary in most grammars and textbooks of Arabic. This form generally serves as the stem to which affixes are added. The form that follows in parentheses is that of the imperfect indicative first person singular. This form is provided to maintain coherence.

kuHuul	alcohol
šaTT lbaHar	beach
tšammas (batšammas)	to sit under the sun
kurat rriiša	badminton
libis (balbis)	to put clothes on
stanna (bastanna)	to wait
ra?san	right away
nbasaT (banibsiT)	to enjoy
musta^{c}id (pl. musta^{c}iddiin)	ready

Other vocabulary found in the following exercises or on tape

msaafir (pl. msaafriin)	a traveler
qiT^{c}a (pl. qiTa^{c})	a passage (in writing)
fihim (bafham)	to understand
^{c}aali	high
?aTa^{c} (ba?Ta^{c})	to cut off, to cross (the river)
Hiwaar (pl. Hiwaaraat)	a dialogue
jaawab (bajaawib)	to answer
t?axxar (bat?axxar)	to be late
Harkat sseer	traffic
ta^{c}liim	education
masraH (pl. masaariH)	a theater
masraHiyya (pl. masraHiyyaat)	a play
rann (i.e., rann ttalafoon)	to ring
?ixtaar (baxtaar)	to choose
taali	following
SaHiiH	correct
?innu	that
?imtiHaan (pl. ?imtiHaanaat)	exams
?awi	strong
haram (pl. ?ahraam)	a pyramid
ma^{c}naa (pl. ma^{c}aani)	meaning
kilma (pl. kilmaat)	a word
qaamuus (pl. qawaamiis)	a dictionary

tamriin 1

jaawib ^{c}ala l?as?ila ttaaliya.

1. ^{c}ala ween raaH Bruce wSandi fi ^{c}uTlat faSil rrabii^{c} ?
2. kam yoom kaanat riHlithum ?
3. ween ?a^{c}adu fi madiinat New York ?
4. kam yoom ?a^{c}adu ^{c}ala TTarii? ?
5. šu ^{c}imlu ?awwal yoom fi New York ?
6. šu šaafu taani yoom fi New York ?
7. ween raaHu taalit yoom fi New York ?
8. leeš ?a^{c}adu fi ?uteel il-YMCA ?
9. ?eemta zaaru Sadii?hum Andy ?
10. kiif kaanat riHlithum ?

tamriin 2

?ixtaar ljawaab SSaHiiH.

1. bnifham min lqiT^{c}a ?innu Bruce wSandy ?a^{c}adu fi New York

    a. xamis ?ayyaam b. ?arba^{c} ?ayyaam c. talat ?ayyaam

2. raaHu Bruce wSandy ^{c}ala New York ^{c}ašaan

    a. yšimmu lhawa b. yzuuru ?ahilhum c. yzuuru SHaabhum

3. saa? ssayyaara min Columbus la New York .... .

    a. Sandy b. Bruce c. Bruce wSandy

4. Sandy wBruce nizlu fi ?uteel l-YMCA .... .

    a. li?annu l?uteel fi wasaT madiinat New York

    b. li?anhum Tullaab

    c. li?annu l?uteel rxiiS

5. bnifham min lqiT^{c}a ?innu .... .

    a. Andy kaan yi^{c}rif ^{c}an riHlit Sandy wBruce ^{c}ala New York min ?abil ma zaaruu.

    b. Andy kaan yi^{c}rif ^{c}an riHlithum ^{c}ala New York bass ma kanš yi^{c}rif ^{c}an ziyaarithum ?ilu.

    c. Andy ma kanš yi^{c}rif ^{c}an riHlithum ?abil ma zaaruu

6. Sandy wBruce .... .

    a. Tullaab min New York b. Tullaab min Ohio

    c. Tullaab byudursu wbyuskunu fi Columbus

tamriin 3

?ixtaar ljawaab SSaHiiH (Review the vocabulary words and their uses in the passage before you do this drill.)

1. limsaafir ^{c}aadatan ... fi ?uteel.
   a. byuskun b. byinzil
2. naaTiHaat ssaHaab ... .
   a. binaayaat ^{c}aalya b. binaayaat zγiira
3. ššams ... kull yoom SSubH.
   a. btiTla^{c} b. bitγiib
4. raaHat Cathy ^{c}ala lmaT^{c}am li?anha kaanat ... .
   a. ta^{c}baana b. joo^{c}aana
5. baštri malaabsi min ... .
   a. maT^{c}am b. maHal tijaari
6. Sadii?ti sihaam ... film fukaahi kull ?usbuu^{c}.
   a. bitzuur b. btuHDur
7. byišrabu nnaas ^{c}aadatan fi lbaar ... .
   b. kuHuul b. ^{c}aSiir burt?aan
8. ... ?axuuy fi maTaar JFK fi New York ?aktar min nuSS see^{c}a lamma ?aja ^{c}ala ?ameerka.
   a. ?a^{c}adt b. stanneet
9. bitruuH rana ^{c}ala šaTT lbaHar ^{c}ašaan ... .
   a. titšammas b. tšuuf ?aSdiqaa?ha
10. ?aTa^{c} yuusuf nahar nniil ... .
   a. maši b. bilma^{c}diyya

tamriin 4

?i?ra lHiwaaraat ttaaliya wjaawib ^{c}ala l?as?ila taHthum.

1. X: kiif kaanat riHiltak ^{c}ala Florida ?
   Y: miš BaTTaala
   X: ?addeeš ?a^{c}adt hunaak ?
   Y: šahreen.
   X: walaaw! haada ma^{c}naa[1] ?innak madarastiš min marra
   Y: ya^{c}ni, darast šwayy.
   su?aal: bnifham min lHiwaar ?innu ... .
   a. Y Taalib b. Y ?ustaaz c. Y muHaami

---

[1] *haada ma^{c}naa* is an idiomatic expression that means "this means."

2. X: šu ^{c}milt fi l^{c}uTla ?

   Y: sabaHt witšammast ktiir.

   su?aal: ween kaan Y fi l^{c}uTla ?

3. X: ?eemta wSilt New York ya muusa ?

   muusa: ssee^{c}a sitta lmaγrib.

   X: leeš t?axxartu ?

   muusa: kaanat Harkat sseer ?awiyya fi maTaar O'Hare fi Chicago.

   su?aal: kiif ?aja muusa ^{c}ala New York ?

li?ann- and ^{c}ašaan

li?ann- does not occur by itself as an independent word in this dialect. A suffixal pronoun is always added to it. Thus, it occurs as *li?anni, li?annak, li?annu, li?anhum,* etc. Sometimes the form *li?annu* is used as a substitute for *li?ann* + any suffixal pronoun, especially when it occurs before *bidd* or *^{c}ind.* When a pronoun is added to *li?annu,* the final suffix -u is dropped. For example, when *-hum* is added to *li?annu* it becomes *li?anhum* not *li?annuhum. li?ann-* is used to express reason. It is usually used at the beginning of the embedded clause, e.g.,

1. nzilt fi ?uteel rxiiS li?anni Taalib wma^{c}iiš fluus ktiira.
2. li?annu ljaww Hilu kull TTullaab byil^{c}abu ttinis.

^{c}ašaan is also used to express reason and occurs at the beginning of an embedded clause. It differs from *li?ann-* with regard to the grammatical category, tense, or mood that follows each:

1. *li?annu* cannot be followed by a subjunctive form. Thus, *ruHt ^{c}ala ljaam^{c}a li?annu ?at^{c}allam* is incorrect in this dialect, whereas *ruHt ^{c}ala ljaam^{c}a ^{c}ašaan ?at^{c}allam* is correct. It can, though, be followed by the indicative and/or perfect forms. *^{c}ašaan,* on the other hand, is usually followed by the subjunctive form of the verb. The perfect and the indicative form of some verb classes such as verbs of emotion and verbs that state facts can follow *^{c}ašaan,* too, e.g.,

   1. ^{c}ašaan binHibb New York ktiir, štareena beet hunaak.
   2. saami Taalib mniiH ^{c}ašaan byudrus ktiir.
   3. ^{c}ašaan saafar xaalid ^{c}ala Chicago, ma ?ajaaš ^{c}ala ljaam^{c}a lyoom.

   It should be noted that in all these examples the use of *li?ann-* is perferable and sounds more authentic and acceptable than *^{c}ašaan.* The fact remains that some native speakers use *^{c}ašaan* and accept it in the above examples.

2. Both *^{c}ašaan* and *li?ann-* can be followed by *bidd, ^{c}ind,* adverbial expressions, preposional phrases, nouns, or pronouns.
3. An adjective can follow *li?ann-* when a suffix is attached to it, but not *^{c}ašaan*.
4. *^{c}ašaan* and *li?ann-* cannot occur in the same sentence in a row.

tamriin 5

?ixtaar ljawaab SSaHiiH.

1. badrus ^{c}arabi li?anni ... .
   a. ?aHibbu ktiir
   b. baHibbu ktiir
   c. biddi ?aHibbu ktiir
   d. ^{c}ašaan ?aHibbu ktiir
2. ?aja xaalid ^{c}ala ?ameerka li?annu ... .
   a. biddu yudrus ^{c}ilm lkumbyuutar
   b. yudrus ^{c}ilm lkumbyuutar
   c. biHubb yudrus ^{c}ilm lkumbyuutar
   d. tta^{c}liim fi ?ameerka mniiH
3. saafart ^{c}ala Florida ^{c}ašaan ... .
   a. bašimm lhawa
   b. ?ašimm lhawa
   c. biddi ?ašimm lhawa
   d. ta^{c}baan ktiir
4. raayHiin ynaamu ^{c}ala Tuul li?anhum ... .
   a. ta^{c}baaniin ktiir
   b. yištiγlu ktiir
   c. štaγalu ktiir
   d. raayHiin yištiγlu ktiir
5. štareet ljariida lyoom ^{c}ašaan ... .
   a. fiiha ?axbaar ktiira
   b. ba?ara l?axbaar
   c. ?a?ara l?axbaar
   d. rxiiSa

tamriin 6

Complete each of the following sentences as you see fit.

1. saafar saami ^{c}ala lbaraaziil li?ann ... .
2. saafarat saamya ^{c}ala Hawaii ^{c}ašaan ... .
3. ma štaraaš Andy sayyaara jdiida li?ann ... .
4. baruuH kull yoom ^{c}ala lmaktaba ^{c}ašaan ... .
5. li?anha sayyaarti btištγilš ... .
6. byitkallam Jim ^{c}arabi mniiH li?ann ... .
7. ^{c}ašaan titkallam ^{c}abla ?ingliizi mniiH ... .
8. biddi ?aruuH ^{c}ala ljaam^{c}a bukra maši li?ann ... .
9. baHubb ?aakul fi maT^{c}am Taj Mahal li?ann ... .
10. biddi ?askun ma^{c} ^{c}eela ^{c}arabiyya ^{c}ašaan ... .

tamriin 7

Give the correct form of the verb given in brackets in each of the following sentences.

1. lamma kunt fi New York ššahar lmaaDi ... ^{c}ala masraH jdiid w ... masraHiyya min masraHiyyaat Shakespeare. (raaH; HaDar)
2. kam wajba ... ?abuuk kull yoom ? (?akal)
3. ?addeeš raayHa ... muna fi lmaTaar ? (stanna)
4. miin Dall ... ma^{c}kum ttinis ba^{c}id ma ruHt ?ana ^{c}ala ššuγul ? (li^{c}ib)
5. ... ?ana wSadii?i l?usbuu^{c} lmaaDi ^{c}ala Chicago w ... fi ?uteel lHoliday Inn ?arba^{c} ?ayyaam. (saafar, ?a^{c}ad) ... maHallaaat ktiira w ... Sadii?na dawu:d (šaaf, zaar).
6. ?eemta badeet ... ^{c}arabi ya Mike ? (t^{c}allam)
7. kiif kaanat riHlitkum ^{c}ala Florida ? ?inšaalla ... ktiir ! (?inbasaT)
8. ?eemta bidkum ... lleela ? (naam)
9. hiyye ^{c}aadatan ... l?axbaar kull yoom ssee^{c}a sitta wnuSS lmaγrib. (tfarraj ^{c}ala)
10. ?addeeš ?a^{c}adtu ... ^{c}ala beet lamma jiitu tudursu fi jaam^{c}it wilaayit Ohio ? (dawwar)

lamma and ?eemta

lamma is a subordination marker used to initiate an embedded clause in a complex sentence. It functions in a way similar to the English subordinator "when." It differs, however, from "when" in that it cannot occur as interrogative word under any circumstance. Thus, sentence (1) below where *lamma* functions as a subordinator is correct, but sentence (2) where *lamma* is used as an interrogative word is not.

1. lamma kunt fi l?urdun zurt lbatra wil^{c}aqaba.
2. lamma zurt lbatra ? meaning presumably "When did you visit Petra?"

?eemta is used in this dialect as an interrogative word. Therefore, substituting *?eemta* for *lamma* in sentence 2 yields a correct sentence, e.g.,

3. ?eemta zurt lbatra ?

tamriin 8

Check whether the following sentences are correct or not and correct the incorrect ones.

1. miin kaan fi lbeet lamma wSilt ? meaning "Who was at home when you arrived?"
2. lamma badat Jane tit^{c}allam ^{c}arabi ? meaning "When did Jane start to learn Arabic?"

3. šu raayiH ti^{c}mal ?eemta bitzuurhum ? meaning "What will you do when visit them?"
4. ween sakanti lamma kunti fi maSir ? meaning "Where did you live when you were in Egypt?"
5. lamma kaanat sayyaarti fi lgaraaj kunt ?aaji ^{c}ala ljaam^{c}a maši kull yoom meaning "When my car was in the garage I used to walk to school every day."
6. ?eemta bada yudrus George ?isbaani kaan ^{c}umru taman sniin meaning "When George began to study Spanish he was eight years old."
7. raayiH ?azuur xamis wilaayaat ?ameerkaaniyya lamma basaafir ^{c}ala ?ameerka ššahar ljaay meaning "I will visit five American states when I travel to the United States next month."
8. rann ttalafoon talat marraat ?eemta kunt naayim meaning "The telephone rang three times when you were asleep."

tamriin 9

Complete the following sentences.

1. lamma kunt ?ana fi New York .... .
2. lamma bat^{c}allam ^{c}arabi mniiH .... .
3. ?akalna samak ktiir lamma .... .
4. lamma štareet ?ana ttilvizyoon jjdiid .... .
5. ?eemta štarat ... ?
6. lamma saafaru ?immi w?abuuy ^{c}ala lmaksiik .... .
7. ?eemta ... fi maT^{c}am ?aaxir marra ?
8. baDall ?adawwir ^{c}ala ma^{c}aani lkalimaat jjdiida fi lqaamuus lamma .... .

Ordinal Numbers

Like English, ordinal numbers in this dialect of Arabic differ in form and use from those of the cardinal ones. The following is a list of both cardinal and ordinal numbers up to twenty.

cardinal alone	cardinal with a noun	ordinal before a noun	ordinal after a noun
waaHad	Taalib waaHad	?awwal Taali	TTaalib l?awwal
(?i)tneen	Taalbeen (?itneen)	taani Taalib	TTaalib ttaani
talaata	talat Tullaab	taalit Taalib	TTaalib ttaalit
?arba^{c}a	?arba^c Tullaab	raabi^c Taalib	TTaalib rraabi^c
xamsa	xamis Tullaab	xaamis Taalib	TTaalib lxaamis

sitta	sitt Tullaab	saadis Taalib	TTaalib ssaadis
sab^{c}a	sabi^{c} Tullaab	saabi^{c} Taalib	TTaalib ssaabi^{c}
tamaanya	taman Tullaab	taamin Taalib	TTaalib ttaamin
tis^{c}a	tisi^{c} Tullaab	taasi^{c} Taalib	TTaalib ttaasi^{c}
^{c}ašara	^{c}ašar Tullaab	^{c}aašir Taalib	TTaalib l^{c}aašir
Hda^{c}š	Hda^{c}ašar Taalib	*	TTaalib liHda^{c}š
?iTna^{c}š	?iTna^{c}šar Taalib	*	TTaalib-i-Tna^{c}š
talatTa^{c}š	talatTa^{c}šar Taalib	*	TTaalib-i-ttalatTa^{c}š
?arba^{c}Tacš	?arba^{c}Ta^{c}šar Taalib	*	TTaalib-i-l?arba^{c}Ta^{c}š
xamisTa^{c}š	xamisTa^{c}šar Taalib	*	TTaalib-i-lxamisTa^{c}š
sitTa^{c}š	sitTa^{c}šar Taalib	*	TTaalib-i-ssitTa^{c}š
saba^{c}Ta^{c}š	saba^{c}Ta^{c}šar Taalib	*	TTaalib-i-ssaba^{c}Ta^{c}š
tamanTa^{c}š	tamanTa^{c}šar Taalib	*	TTaalib-i-ttamanTa^{c}š
tisi^{c}Ta^{c}š	tisi^{c}Ta^{c}šar Taalib	*	TTaalib-i-tisi^{c}Ta^{c}š
^{c}išriin	^{c}išriin Taalib	*	TTaalib l^{c}išriin

tamriin 10

Based on this table, form the rules that determine noun-number association in this dialect of Arabic. The following rule is given as an example for illustration:

-ar is added to the cardinal numbers 11-19 in number-noun phrases.

* Instructor will discuss the answers with you in class

tamriin 11

Write down the correct form of the number-noun given in brackets for each sentence below.

1. štarat salwa mbaariH .... . (fifteen books)
2. saafar ^{c}ali ma^{c} ... ^{c}ala lhind ?abil yoomeen. (three students)
3. biddi ?askun ma^{c} ... btudrus ^{c}arabi fi ljaam^{c}a. (one female student)
4. darasu TTullaab ... l?usbuu^{c} lmaaDi. (the fifth book)
5. fi ... min riHlitna ^{c}ala Chicago šufna Sears Tower wWater Tower. (sixth day)
6. štaγalt ^{c}ala lkumbyuutar .... . (five days)
7. kull ... baruuH ^{c}ala likniisa ^{c}ašaan ?ašuuf ?aSdiqaa?i/sadaay?i. (fifth day)
8. tγadeet yoom lxamiis lmaaDi ma^{c} ... ?aju min ssa^{c}uudiyya ^{c}ašaa yudursu hoon (two. female students)

tamriin 12

Use each of the following words and expressions in a meaningful sentence of your own.

fi l?axiir, ^{c}ala Tuul, ra?san, musta^{c}id, Taali^{c}, min ... la, Hatta, joo^{c}aan, ta^{c}baan.

Dall and ?a^{c}ad

Both *Dall* and *?a^{c}ad* have more than one meaning and use. One of these uses is to express the past progressive action. They usually precede other verbs when used to express progressive actions, e.g.,

1. Dallat widaad tudrus Tuul lleel "Widad went on studying all night long."
2. ?a^{c}dat widaad tudrus Tuul lleel "Widad went on studying all night long."

In this context they can be used interchangeably, and the verb that comes after each is in the subjunctive form.

tamriin 13

Complete the following sentences.

1. lamma zurna ^{c}eelit zooj/ti ?a^{c}adna .... .
2. šu Dalleetu ... kull l?usbuu^{c} hunaak ?
3. Dalleet mbaariH ... fi lmaktaba min ssee^{c}a ^{c}ašara SSubuH la ssee^{c}a xamsa lmaɣrib.
4. ?a^{c}dat miryam ... la muddit talat see^{c}aat yoom ljum^{c}a lmaaDi.
5. Dall Jim w?uxtu ... ^{c}ala ttilvizyoon Tuul lleel.
6. ?addeeš raayiH tu^{cc}ud ... ?

taani

aani has two meanings: the ordinal number "second" and "another," e.g.,

1. ma šuftiš Sadii?i saami fi New York fi riHilti l?axiira, bass raayiH ?ašuufu fi riHla taanya nšaalla. (another)
2. ma šuftiš Sadii?i saami fi New York fi riHilti l?axiira, bass raayiH ?ašuufu fi rriHla ttaanya nšaalla (second, next)
3. ?areet ktaab taani ^{c}an taariix ?ooroobba ?abil yoomeen. (another)
4. ?areet liktaab ttaani ^{c}an taariix ?ooroobba ?abil yoomeen. (second)

The meaning of *taani* as "second" or "another" is determined by word order and definiteness: (1) indefinite *taani* preceded by an indefinite noun tends to mean "another"; (2) indefinite *taani* followed by an indefinite noun means "second"; and (3) definite *taani* preceded by a definite noun means either "second," "next," "following," or "other." The intended meaning in (3) is detemined by the context.

tamriin 14

Determine the meaning of *taani* in each of the following sentences.

1. ?a^{c}Tiini ktaab taani, min faDlak!
2. taani Tayyaara nizlit ?abil see^{c}a.
3. taani ?usbuu^{c} darasna ^{c}an taariix maSir bass.
4. xud ssayyaara ttaanya.
5. raayHiin nšuuf l?ahraam fi l?usbuu^{c} ttaani.
6. wiSil TTaalib ttaani ?abil ?usbuu^{c}.

tamriin 15

Write three separate sentences on each use of *taani.*

tamriin 16

1. Describe the trip you have or you would have liked to have taken over the spring break.
2. Rewrite the story "riHla ^{c}ala New York" using the pronoun *?iHna* instead of *humme*.

Listen to Tape Segment #20

^{c}adnaan biddu ysaafir ^{c}ala ?usturaalya

^{c}adnaan:	marHaba.
wakiil ssafar:	?ahlan wsahlan, ?ayy xidma ya ?ax ?
^{c}adnaan:	biddi ?aštri tazkarat safar ^{c}ala ?usturaalya ^{c}ašaan ?aHDur mu?tamar.
wakiil ssafar:	tfaDDal stariiH. ?eemta biddak tsaafir ?
^{c}adnaan:	ba^{c}id šahreen.
wakiil ssafar:	min ?ayy madiina biddak tiTla^{c} wween biddak tinzil fi?usturaalya ?
^{c}adnaan:	biddi ?aTla^{c} min dimašq w?anzil fi Adelaide.
wakiil ssafar:	laHZa min faDlak. fiš ^{c}indna riHlaat la Adelaide, bass fi ^{c}indna riHlaat la Sydney. šu raayak ?
^{c}adnaan:	wkiif raayiH ?asaafir min Sydney la Adelaide ?
wakiil ssafar:	bitsaafir bilbaaS ?aw bilbaaxra.
^{c}adnaan:	?addeeš ?ujrit lbaaS w?addeeš ?ujrit lbaaxra ?
wakiil ssafar:	?inta biddak tazkara raayiH-jaay willa raayiH bass ?
^{c}adnaan:	biddi tazkara raayiH-jaay.
wakiil ssafar:	?inta Taalib ?
^{c}adnaan:	la?, ?ana miš Taalib.

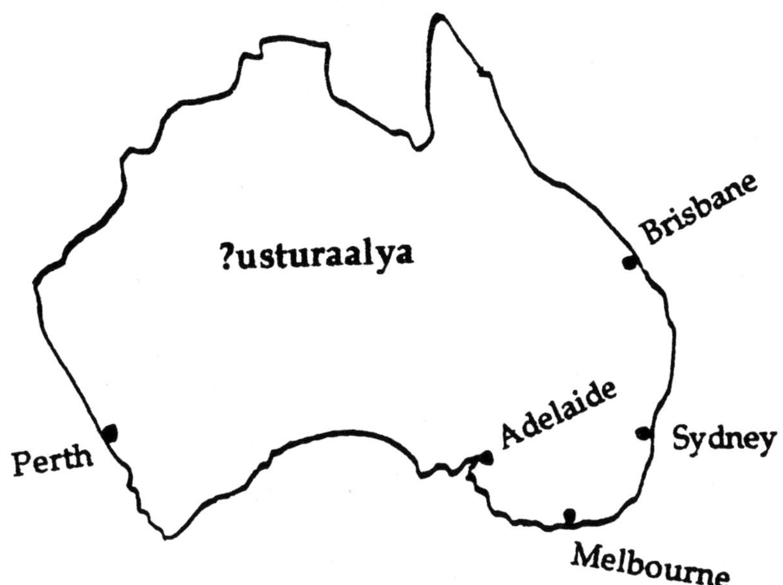

wakiil ssafar: ?addeeš ^{c}umrak ? ?iza ^{c}umrak ?a?al min 26 sana bti?dar tištri tazkara bsi^{c}ir TTullaab, bass ?iza ^{c}umrak ?aktar min 26 sana bti?darš.

^{c}adnaan: ^{c}umri 28 sana, bass miš muhim ^{c}indi si^{c}ir ttazkara. šširka ?illi baštγil fiiha raayiHa tidfa^{c} ttakaaliif.

wakiil ssafar: mumtaaz, ?izan. biddak ?iyyaaha fi ddaraja l?uula willa fi ddaraja ttaanya.

^{c}adnaan: ?addeeš lfar? fi ssi^{c}ir been ddaraja l?uula widdaraja ttaanya ?

wakiil ssafar: fii far? kbiir, Hawaali sit miit leera.

^{c}adnaan: haada fi^{c}lan far? kbiir. xalliiha ?izan daraja taanya.

wakiil ssafar: ?inta bitdaxxin willa la? ?

^{c}adnaan: la? ?ana badaxxinš.

wakiil ssafar: bitHubb tu^{cc}ud janb ššubbaak willa janb lmamar ?

^{c}adnaan: baHubb ?a^{cc}ud janb ššubbaak.

wakiil ssafar: haadi ttazkara. raayiH tiTla^{c} min maTaar dimašq ddawli ssee^{c}a ^{c}ašara wrubu^{c} SSubH. btaSal New Delhi ssee^{c}a sitta wnuSS lmaγrib. btinzil TTayyaara fi maTaar New Delhi limuddat see^{c}a wnuSS. btiTla^{c} min maTaar New Delhi ssee^{c}a tamaanya lmaγrib. btaSal Sydney taani yoom ssee^{c}a sab^{c}a SSubuH. btaaxud lbaaS ?aw lbaaxra la Adelaide fi nafs lyoom ?aw taani yoom. bikalfak lbaaS tis^{c}iin duulaar raayiH jaay wilbaaxra bitkallif 120 duulaar. ^{c}indak ?ayy su?aal taani ?

^{c}adnaan: leeš biTawwil ssaffra ktiir ?

wakiil ssafar: li?annu fi far? beenna wbeen ?usturaalya saba^{c} see^{c}aat.

^{c}adnaan: Tayyib, ?eemta laazam ?akuun fi lmaTaar ?abil ma tiTla^{c} TTayyaara ?

wakiil ssafar: laazim tkuun hunaak ?abil ma tiTla^{c} TTayyaara bsee^{c}teen.

^{c}adnaan: bti?balu šekkaat hoon ?

wakiil ssafar: Tab^{c}an

^{c}adnaan: haada šekk bi?alf wmiit leera.

wakiil ssafar: šukran. riHla mwaffa?a, nšaalla.

^{c}adnaan: šukran.

lmufradaat

wakiil safar	travel agent
tazkara (pl. tazaakir)	a ticket
stariiH	be seated, have a seat
HaDar (baHDur)	to attend
mu?tamar	a conference
Tili^{c} (baTla^{c})	to take off
nizil (banzil)	to land
?ujra	wage, charge
raayiH	going
jaay	coming
tazkara raayiH-jaay	two-way ticket
tazkara raayiH bass	one-way ticket

?idir (ba?dar)	can, to be able to
?a?al (comp. from ?aliil)	less than
miš muhim	it does not matter; it is not important
taklifa (pl. takaaliif)	cost, expense
daraja	class, degree
daraja ?uula	first class
daraja taanya	economy class
far?	difference
fi^{c}lan	real
xalla (baxalli)	to let it be
laHZa	a moment
laHZa, min faDlak	a moment, please!
baaxra (pl. bawaaxir)	ship
?iza	if
daxxan (badaxxin)	to smoke
mamar (pl. mamarraat)	aisle
dawli	international
Tawwal (baTawwil)	to take a long time
safra	trip
laazim	must
?ibil (ba?bal)	to accept
nafs	same, self
riHla mwaffa?a	have a nice trip!
taman	price, value
xidma (pl. xidmaat)	service
?ayy xidma ya ?ax ?	Can I help you? What can I do for you?

Other vocabulary found in the following exercises or on tape

massal (bamassil)	to represent
mubaašir	direct
musbaqan	in advance
šufeer (pl. šufariyya)	a driver
maHalli	local
sa?al (bas?al)	to ask
ribiH (barbaH)	to win
lyaanaSiib	lottery
xaaSS	special

dafac (badfac)	to pay
macluumaat	information
xallaS (baxalliS)	to finish
mamnuuc	forbidden
masmuuH	allowed
siigaara	cigarette
llid	Lod

tamriin 1

jaawib cala l?as?ila ttaaliya.

1. cala ween biddu ysaafir cadnaan ?
2. ?eemta biddu ysaafir ?
3. ?addeeš cumur cadnaan ?
4. min ?ayy maTaar biddu ysaafir ?
5. cala ?ayy madiina fi ?usturaalya biddu ysaafir ?
6. miin raayiH yidfac takaaliif riHiltu ?
7. ?addeeš sicir ttazkara ?illi ?ištraraaha cadnaan ?
8. ?eemta raayiH yiTlac cadnaan min maTaar dimašq ?
9. ?eemta raayiH yaSal Sydney ?
10. kiif raayiH ysaafir min Sydney la Adelaide ?
11. šu nooc ttazkara ?illi ?ištaraaha ?
12. leeš bitTawwil rriHla ktiir been dimašq wSydney ?
13. ween biHibb yuccud cadnaan ?
14. kam siigaara bidaxxin cadnaan fi lyoom ?
15. kiif dafac taman ttazkara ?

tamriin 2

?ixtaar ljawwaab SSaHiiH.

1. bnifham min lHiwaar ?innu cadnaan biddu ysaafir cala ?usturaalya cašaan ... .
   a. yšimm lhawa b. yzuur ?aSHaabu
   c. ymassil širiktu
2. raayiH yinzil cadnaan fi Sydney li?annu ... .
   a. fiš riHlaat min dimašq mubaašira la Adelaide
   b. fiš maTaar fi Adelaide
   c. ttazkara min dimašq la Sydney rxiiSa ktiir
3. raayiH ysaafir cadnaan min Sydney la Adelaide ... .
   a. bilbaaS b. bilbaaxra c. bilbaaS ?aww lbaaxra

4. si^{c}ir ttazkara ma kanš muhim ^{c}ind ^{c}adnaan li?annu
   a. biHubb ysaafir ^{c}ala ?usturaalya
   b. ^{c}umru 28 sana
   c. širkitu raayHa tidfa^{c} taman ttazkara
5. biddu yu^{cc}ud ^{c}adnaan janb ššubbaak li?annu .... .
   a. bidaxxinš b. štara tazkara fi ddaraja ttaanya
   c. biHubb yu^{cc}ud janb ššubbaak
6. btaaxud rriHla min dimašq la Sydney .... .
   a. 20:^{45} see^{c}a b. 13:^{45} see^{c}a c. 21:^{00} see^{c}a
7. štara ^{c}adnaan tazkara fi ddaraja ttaanya li?annu .... .
   a. ttazkara ?arxaS min ddaraja l?uula
   b. šširka raayHa tidfa^{c} taman ttazkara
   c. biHubb yu^{cc}ud ^{c}adnaan fi ddaraja ttaanya

tamriin 3

?ixtaar ljawaab SSaHiiH (Review the vocabulary words and their uses in the passage before attempting to answer the questions in this exercise.)

1. TTayyaara ^{c}aadatan ... fi lmaTaar.
   a. btinzil b. btiTla^{c}
2. lamma binsaafir bittaksi laazim .... .
   a. ništri tazkara musbaqan b. nidfa^{c} ?ujrit ttaksi laššufeer
3. lamma baštri tazkara raayiH-jaay ^{c}ala lbaraaziil .... .
   a. basaafir ^{c}ala lbaraaziil wbarja^{c} min hunaak
   b. basaafir ^{c}ala lbaraaziil wbaDall hunaak
4. ttazkara fi ddaraja l?uula ^{c}aadatan ... min ttazkara fi ddaraja ttaanya.
   a. ?arxaS b. ?aγla
5. biHubb yu^{cc}ud yuusuf janb lmamar fi TTayyaara. ma^{c}naa mamar ...
   a. ššubbaak b. TTarii?
6. maTaar John F. Kennedy fi madiinat New York .... .
   a. maHalli b. dawli
7. ... liktaab 25 jneeh.
   a. taman b. far?
8. ... šekkaat fi lmaT^{c}am.
   a. byi?daru b. byi?balu

Conditional Sentences

Conditionals are a complex issue in this dialect. Native speakers often find themselves unable to pinpoint or even to realize differences in meaning between similar conditional sentences. Despite this complexity, some rudimentary regularities can be found:

1. There are two conditional particles in this dialect, *?iza* and *law*. *?iza* tends to indicate that an action is probable, and *law* indicates that an action is not probable or even possible in some cases. Thus, conditionals in this dialect of Arabic are different from English where tense determines whether the action is probable or not.

2. Both perfect and imperfect tenses can be used in conditonal clauses. The choice of one tense over another is determined by the meaning for **some** speakers. Consider the following four sentences and their meanings.

a. ?iza barbaH lyaanaSiib baštri beet jdiid.

barbaH is in the imperfect. The sentence can be rendered into "If I win the lottery, I will buy a new house."

b. ?iza rbiHt lyaanaSiib baštri beet jdiid.

rbiHt is in the imperfect and conveys the same meaning as in (1) but requires a different context than (1) The proper context for this sentence is one in which the winning numbers have been announced but not known to the interlocuters.

In both sentences *?iza* has been used. In both cases it indicates that the act in the main clause is probable if the condition is met, and there is nothing in the sentence to show why the condition cannot be met.

c. law barbaH lyaanaSiib baštri beet jdiid.

barbaH is in the imperfect. The sentence conveys the sense of wishing. It can be rendered into "It is unlikely that I will win the lottery and buy a new house, but I am not completely hopeless."

d. law rbiHt lyaanaSiib, la štareet beet jdiid.

Both *rbiHt* and *štareet* are in the perfect. The sentence indicates that it is too late to win the lottery and buy a new house. Thus, it is impossible for the act to happen.

In some cases changing the tense does not lead to a change in meaning. For example, 83% of native speakers[1] do not see any difference in meaning between sentences e and f below though the tense in e is imperfect and in f perfect.

[1]This outcome is based on a survey conducted on 36 native speakers who were asked to judge the grammaticality of some conditionals and to pinpoint meaning differences as they perceived them.

e. ?iza biSiir ma^{c}i fluus ktiira baštri beet jdiid.

f. ?iza Saar ma^{c}i fluus ktiira baštri beet jdiid.

Both sentences mean that "If I become (one day) rich, I will buy a new house." However, sentence e is usually more acceptable and apparently more commonly used than sentence f. Some native speakers judge sentence f as understood, occasionally used, incorrect, but acceptable.

In short, there are two conditional particles in this dialect, *?iza* and *law*. *?iza* is used to convey an action that is probable, and *law* conveys an action that is usually improbable, but it *(law)* may also convey the sense of wishing, blaming, suggesting. Tense alteration in conditional sentences reflect, at times, delicate and subtle differences in meaning. This difference is not always perceived by the average native speaker.

tamriin 4

Combine each of the two following clauses given below using either *?iza* or *law*. Make the necessary changes in tense to fit the intended meaning.

1. bitsaafir Carol ^{c}ala maSir. btit^{c}allam ^{c}arabi mniiH.
2. ^{c}indi fluus ktiira. baštri beet kbiir.
3. byinzil saami fi ?uteel lHilton. byidfa^{c} saami fluus ktiira.
4. binšuuf burj ?iifil fi baariis. ?iHna binsaafir ^{c}ala faransa.
5. miš raayHa tit^{c}allam Jane ^{c}arabi mniiH. Jane bitDall fi Columbus.

tamriin 5

Complete each of the following sentences. Make sure to maintain the coherence of the meaning.

1. ?iza badrus ^{c}ašar see^{c}aat kull yoom .... .
2. law barbaH lyaanaSiib .... .
3. btaakli ?akil ^{c}arabi ?iza .... .
4. raayHa naadya tisbaH wtitšammas ktiir law.... .
5. ?iza baruHš ^{c}ala ljaam^{c}a SSeef ljaay .... .

?illi

?illi is a relative word comparable in its use to the English relative words who, that, which, and whom. It is used to introduce a subordinate clause in a complex sentence, e.g.,

liktaab ?illi štareetu mbaariH Sa^{c}ib ktiir.

ma šuftiš TTullaab lijdaad ?illi byudursu ^{c}arabi fi jaam^{c}it baγdaad.

?illi is always preceded by a definite noun. A resumptive pronoun referring to the noun appears at the end of the embedded clause when (1) the verb in the embedded clause is transitive, and (2) this noun has been extracted from the object position.

tamriin 6

Combine each of the two sentences in the following list using *?illi.*

1. ?ana baakul ?akil ^{c}arabi fi maT^{c}am. lmaT^{c}am fi šaari^{c} High.
2. Sara btištγll fi maktab safar. maktab ssafar fi TTaabi? ttaani.
3. haada Sadii?i. huwwe byištγil ?ustaaz fi jaam^{c}it wilaayit Ohio.
4. šuft ?ustaaz l^{c}arabi. huwwe byuskun janb lmustašfa.
5. štaγalt fi maT^{c}am lamuddat šahreen. lmaT^{c}am fi šaari^{c} Lane.
6. jamaal byuskun fi beet. lbeet janb madrasatna.
7. ?iHna binHibb naakul HummuS. ?immi bti^{c}mal lHummuS.
8. ?ana ba^{c}rafš ?asuu? ssayyaara. ?inta bitsuu? ssayyaara.

tamriin 7

Fill in the blanks.

1. haada ... ?illi byudrus taariix fi jaami^{c}at Chicago.
2. kaan lfilm ?illi šufnaa mbaariH ... .
3. štara nabiil (male's name) kull lkutub ?illi ... .
4. ljaam^{c}a ?illi badrus fiiha ... .
5. ba^{c}rafš ?ism TTaalba ?illi ... .
6. ma šuftiš kull l?aflaam l^{c}arabiyya ?illi ... .
7. TTaalib lyuunaani ?illi byuskun ma^{c}na ... .
8. ?aHmad ... ljaww ?illi maaTir daayman.

tamriin 8

Construct eight meaningful sentences from the following table.

	?ana	saafar		lqaahira
	?aHmad	štara ?amiiS	fi	maTaar New York
bidd	warda	riji^{c}	min	lmaksiik
laazim	humme	nizil	janb	J. C. Penny
	Jim	Tili^{c}	^{c}ala	San Francisco
	?inti	sakan	^{c}an	Sears

Examples of these sentences are

1. biddu ?aHmad ysaafir ᶜala lmaksiik.
2. laazim ?anzil fi maTaar New York

tamriin 9

Listen to the instructions concerning this ticket on tape.

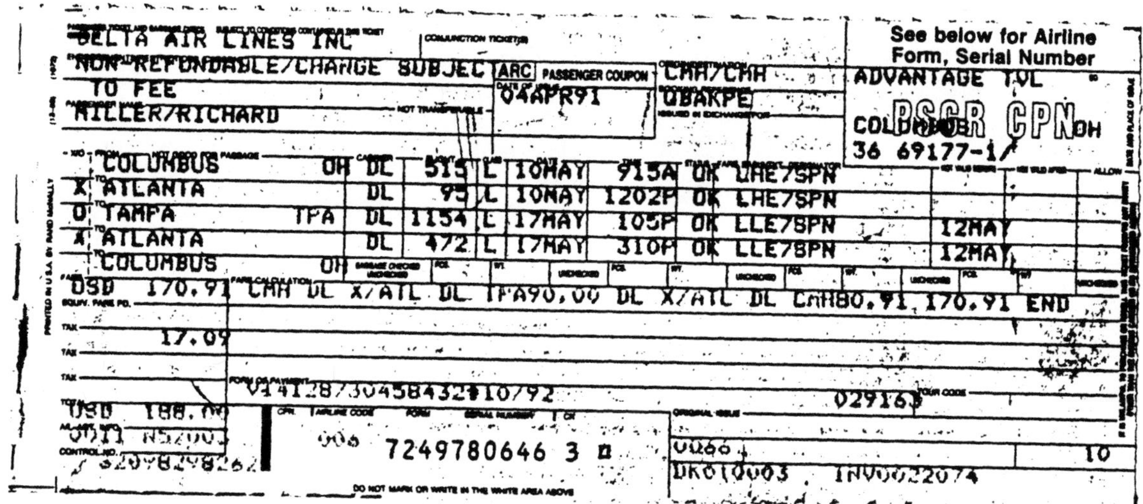

DELTA AIR LINES INC
NON-REFUNDABLE/CHANGE SUBJECT TO FEE
ARC PASSENGER COUPON
04APR91
CMH/CMH
UBAKPE
MILLER/RICHARD

See below for Airline Form, Serial Number
ADVANTAGE TVL
COLUMBUS OH
PSGR CPN
36 69177-1

	COLUMBUS	OH	DL	515	L	10MAY	915A	OK	LHE7SPN	
X	ATLANTA		DL	95	L	10MAY	1202P	OK	LHE7SPN	
O	TAMPA	TPA	DL	1154	L	17MAY	105P	OK	LLE7BPN	12MAY
X	ATLANTA		DL	472	L	17MAY	310P	OK	LLE7BPN	12MAY
	COLUMBUS	OH								

USD 170.91 CMH DL X/ATL DL TPA90.00 DL X/ATL DL CMH80.91 170.91 END

TAX 17.09

V141287304584321 10/92

029163

USD 188.00

006 7249780646 3

0066

DK010003 INV0022074

10

DO NOT MARK OR WRITE IN THE WHITE AREA ABOVE

Listen toTape Segment #21

fi l^{c}iyaada

lmariiD: marHaba!

ddaktoor: ?ahleen. xeer! šu maalak ?

lmariiD: rukubti btooja^{c}ni.

ddaktoor: ?addeeš Saarilha btooj^{c}ak ?

lmariiD: talat ?ayyaam.

ddaktoor: bti^{c}raf ssabab ? bti^{c}raf leeš btooj^{c}ak ?

lmariiD: ?aywa. kunt ?al^{c}ab kurat lqadam ma^{c} ?aSHaabi ?abil talat ?ayyaam. wiHna nil^{c}ab w?i^{c}t ^{c}ala rukubti wba^{c}deen Saarat tooja^{c}ni.

ddaktoor: šuft ?ayy daktoor taani ?

lmariiD: la?.

ddaktoor: Tayyib, xalliini ?afHaSha.

* * * * *

ddaktoor: muškilatak basiiTa, ma ti?la?š.

lmariiD: šu lmuškila ya daktoor ?

ddaktoor: raDDa basiiTa. raayHa TTiib ba^{c}id ?usbuu^{c} nšaalla. ^{c}ala ?ayyit Haal, raayiH ?a^{c}Tiik rušeeta ^{c}ašaan tištri dawa.

lmariiD: min ?ayy Saydaliyya baštri ddawa ?

ddaktoor: ?aah .... baZunn Saydaliyyat ššifaa?[1] ?a?rab Saydaliyya ^{c}aleena. b^{c}iida d?ii?teen maši min hoon. ?iTla^{c} min hoon wduur ^{c}ala lyamiin fi šaari^{c} l^{c}awda. ?imši duɣri Hawaali miiteen mitir. Saydaliyyat ššifaa? bitkuun ^{c}ala yamiinak janb sinama lwaliid. mniiH ?

lmariiD: šukran duktoor. ?addeeš btu?mur ?

ddaktoor: xamis danaaniir, min faDlak.

lmariid: tfaDDal.

ddaktoor: šukran. biššifaa? nšaalla.

lmariiD: šukran.

fi SSaydaliyya

lmariiD: ?assalaamu ^{c}alaykum!

SSaydali: wa^{c}alaykum ssalaam! šu btu?mur ya ?ax ?

lmariiD: biddi ?aštri dawa larukubti.

SSaydali: ma^{c}ak rušeeta ?

lmariiD: na^{c}am. tfaDDal!

SSaydali: tfaDDal strariiH ^{c}ala lkursi, halla baHaDDirlak ?iyyaa.

lmariiD: ?addeeš byaaxud taHDiirhu ?

SSaydali: ^{c}ašar da?aayi? ^{c}ala l?aktar.

lmariiD: Tayyib wala yhimmak.

---

[1]Sayydaliyyat ššifaa?, šaari^{c} l^{c}awda, and sinama lwaliid are all proper names that refer to a pharmacy, a street, and a movie theater, respectively.

(ba^{c}d ^{c}ašar da?aayi?)

SSaydali: tfaDDal! ddawa jaahiz. btaaxud talat Habbaat kul yoom. Habba ba^{c}id lifTuur wHabba ba^{c}id lɣada wHabba ba^{c}id l^{c}aša. ?iza btitHassanš b^{c}id talat ?ayyaam, ?irja^c ^{c}ala ddaktoor ?illi ?a^{c}Taak rrušeeta w?iza tHassant kammil l^{c}ilaaj Hatta yuxluS ddawa. fhimt ^{c}alay ?

lmariiD: fhimt. btinSaHni ši taani ?

SSaydali: ?aywa. timšiiš ktiir, Haawil tistariiH ?adar l?imkaan.

lmariiD: šukran. ?addeeš btu?mur ya ?ax ?

SSaydali: l?amir lilaah. dinaar wnuSS.

lmariiD: tfaDDal, hayy dinaar wnuSS.

SSaydali: šukran, biššifaa? nšaalla.

lmariiD: šukran.

lmufradaat

^{c}iyaada	clinic
mariiD	patient, sick, ill
xeer	good news, I hope!
šu maalak ?	what's the matter?
rukba	knee
wajja^c (bawajji^c)	to hurt, to cause pain
sabab	reason, cause
wi?i^c (ba?a^c)	to fall down
Saar (baSiir)	to become, to start
faHaS (bafHaS)	to check
basiiT	simple, small
ma ti?la?š	don't worry
raDDa	a bruise
Taab (baTiib)	to recover
nšaalla	God willing!
^{c}ala ?ayyit Haal	however
rušeeta	prescription
dawa (pl. ?adwiya)	medicine
Zann (baZunn)	to think, to believe
Saydaliyya	pharmacy
šifaa?	recovery
?a?rab	the closest

waliid	Arabic proper name
?amar (ba?mur)	to order
?addeeš btu?mur ?	how much do you order (charge)?
biššifaa? nšaalla	I wish you recovery
HaDDar (baHaDDir)	to prepare
^{c}ala l?aktar	at the most
wala yhimmak	don't worry
jaahiz	ready
Habba (pl. Habbaat)	pill, tablet
tHassan (batHassan)	to improve
kammal (bakammil)	to continue
^{c}ilaaj	treatment
^{c}aalaj (ba^{c}aalij)	to treat
naSaH (banSaH)	to recommend, to advise
Haawal (baHaawil)	to try
?adar l?imkaan	as much as possible
l?amir lilaah	a compliment meaning literally "order be to God"
hayy	abbreviation for haada

Other vocabulary found in the following exercises or on tape

wa?it	time
di??a	accuracy
faayda	use
biduun	without
t^{c}arraf ^{c}ala (bat^{c}arraf)	to meet, to get introduced to
kahraba	electricity
?in?aTa^{c}	was/were cut off
daxal (badxul)	to enter
liSS (pl. luSuuS)	a thief
^{c}abiir	Arabic female's name
daa?ira	department
marawaana	marijuana
bsur^{c}a	at a speed of
masak (bamsik)	to catch
kafitiirya	cafeteria
Haadis sayyaara	car accident
ta?miin	insurance

Additional necessary vocabulary

maraD (pl. ?amraaD)	disease
?alam (pl. ?aalaam)	pain
?iltihaab	infection
?intifaax	swelling
jurH (pl. jruuH)	a wound
kasir (pl. ksuur)	a fracture
^{c}aDim (pl. ^{c}Daam)	a bone
Suddaa^{c}	headache
?imsaak	constipation
?ishaal	diarrhea
?aHHa/sa^{c}al	cough
rašiH	cold
fluwanza	flu
Hamaawa	fever
dooxa	dizziness
bard	stomach flu
Hasaasiyya	allergy
?urHa	an ulcer
?amraaD jinsiyya	sexually transmitted diseases

tamriin 1 (?as?ila)

1. leeš raaH lmariiD ^{c}ala ddaktoor ?
2. kiif Saarat lmuškila ?
3. ?addeeš Saarliha rukubtu btooji^{c} ?
4. ween Saydaliyyit ššifaa? ?
5. ?addeeš dafa^{c} lmariiD laddaktoor ?
6. ?addeeš btaaxud wa?it ^{c}ašaan yHaDDir SSaydali ddawa ?
7. ?eemta laazim yaaxud lmariiD ddawa ?
8. ?iza bitHassanš lmariiD ba^{c}id talat ?ayyaam, šu laazim yi^{c}mal ?
9. ?addeeš si^{c}ir ddawa ?
10. ?iza bitHassan lmariiD, šu laazim yi^{c}mal ?

tamriin 2

?ixtaar ljawaab SSaHiiH.

1. Saarat rukbit lmariiD tooj^{c}u li?annu ... .

   a. kaan yil^{c}ab kurat lqadam b. wi?i^{c} ^{c}aleeha

c. šaaf daktoor taani

2. biTTiib rukbit lmariiD ba^{c}id ?usbuu^c ?iza .... .

   a. byaaxud lmariiD ddawa   b. byimšiiš ^{c}aleeha ktiir

   c. byimšiiš ^{c}aleeha ktiir wibyaaxud ddawa

3. raaH lmariiD ^{c}ala Saydaliyyit ššifaa? li?anha .... .

   a. ?a?rab Saydaliyya ^{c}ala ^{c}iyaadat ddaktoor

   b. janb sinama lwaliid

   c. Saydaliyya mniiHa ktiir

4. SSaydaliyya fi šaari^c .... .

   a. ššifaa?   b. lwaliid   c. l^{c}awda

5. laazim yaaxud lmariiD .... .

   a. talat Habbaat dawa ba^{c}id lifTuur kull yoom

   b. Habteen, waHada ba^{c}id lɣada wwaHada ba^{c}id l^{c}aša bass

   c. Habba waHada ba^{c}id lifTuur

6. lmariiD dafa^c laddaktoor wSSaydali .... .

   a. xamis danaaniir   b. sitt danaaniir wnuSS   c. dinaar wnuSS

tamriin 3

?ixtaar ljawaab SSaHiiH (Review the vocabulary words and their correct uses before you start this.)

1. lmariiD biruuH ^{c}aadatan ^{c}ala ... fi l?awwal.

   a. l^{c}iyaada   b. SSaydaliyya

2. byištru nnaas ^{c}aadatan ddawa min .... .

   a. ddaktoor   b. SSaydaliyya

3. ?illi byiHaDDir ddawa ^{c}aadatan .... .

   a. ddaktoor   b. SSaydali

4. ?illi byaaxud ddawa ^{c}aadatan .... .

   a. lmariiD   b. ddaktoor

5. kaan ddaktoor ... lamriiD lamma šuftu.

   a. yifHaS   b. yHaawil

6. lamma ddaktor bya^{c}Ti lmariiD l^{c}ilaaj laazim lmariiD .... .

   a. yinSaHu   b. yxalSu

W- (pronounced either /u/ or /w/ depending on the following sound)

We have covered two main uses for *w-* so far. One use is as a coordinator that conjoins two constituents (i.e., nouns, verbs, clauses, sentences, etc.) in a compound or simple sentence. In this sense it is similar in its use to "and" in English, e.g.,

1. ruHt ^{c}ala ssuu? mbaariH wištareet badla. (two clauses)
2. hiyaam w?amal zaaruuni l?usbuu^{c} lmaaDi. (two nouns)
3. lamma wSilt lbeet ?akalt wnimt ^{c}ala Tuul. (two verbs)
4. jaawab fariid ^{c}ala ssu?aal bsur^{c}a wbidi??a. (two adverbs)

The other use is as a subordinator that relates two clauses in a complex sentence similar to the use of "while" or "as" in English. The following examples illustrate its use as a relative subordinator:

1. w?ana fi New York zurt timsaal lHuriyya.
2. ?aabalat muna rra?iis Saddam Hussein whiyye fi baɣdaad.

w- as a subordinator is always followed by a noun or a pronoun. It cannot be followed directly by a verb as is the case with *lamma*. The subordinating clause that follows *w-* can have an imperfect verb or a subjunctive, but not a perfect verb. It can also be a verbless clause (i.e., equational clause) or have an active participle such as *naayim, raayiH, ?aa^{c}id*.

tamriin 4

Combine each of the following sentences into one sentence using *w-*.

1. ^{c}ali kaan fi Florida. ^{c}ali raaH ^{c}ala Disney World.
2. Tom kaan yudrus fi Ohio State. Tom t^{c}arraf ^{c}ala Debbie.
3. rann ttalafoon talat marraat. ^{c}abla (kaanat) naayma.
4. kunt ?adrus fi TTaabi? ttaani fi lmaktaba. ?aja ^{c}alay ?axuuy.
5. humme bitfarraju ^{c}ala ttilvizyoon. lkahraba ?in?aT^{c}at.

tamriin 5

?ixtaar ljawaab SSaHiiH.

1. daxal lliSS lbeet wJane .... .
   a. kaanat titfarraj ^{c}ala attilvizyoon b. btitfarraj ^{c}ala ttilvizyoon
   c. titfarraj ^{c}ala ttilvizyoon d. tfarrajat ^{c}ala ttilvizyoon
2. t^{c}allamt ^{c}arabi mniiH w?ana .... .
   a. kunt fi l?urdun b. sakant ma^{c} ^{c}abiir
   c. fi maSir d. ?aštɣil fi daa?irat l^{c}arabi
3. wiHna ... masakna lbuliis.
   a. šribna kuHuul fi ššaari^{c} b. kunna ndaxxin marawaana
   c. nsuu? bsur^{c}it 75 miil fi ssee^{c}a
4. t^{c}arraft ^{c}ala ?amal whiyye .... .
   a. Taaliba fi jaami^{c}at Ohio State b. darsat fi jaami^{c}at Michigan
   c. kaanat tištiɣil fi lkafitiirya d. til^{c}ab ma^{c}na ttinis

Parts of the Body

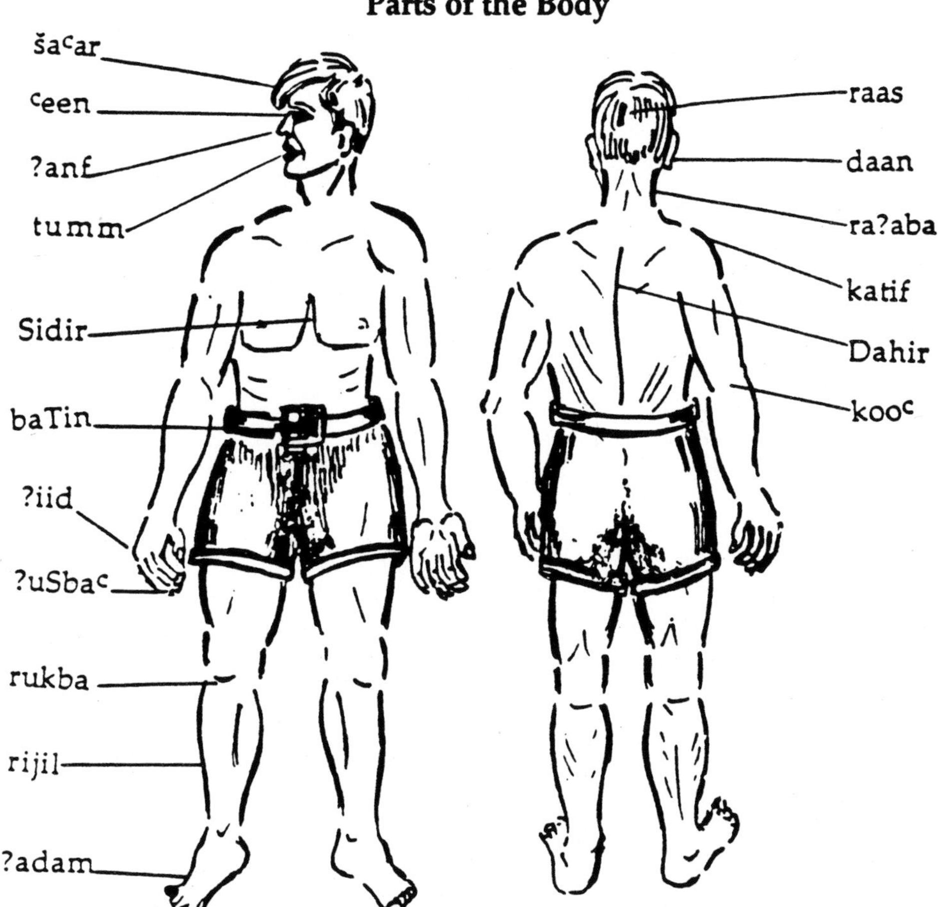

Elative Adjectives

This dialect of Arabic has two forms of adjectives: the base (positive) and the elative. The elative form combines comparative and superlative adjectives. The elative form conveys the comparative meaning when it is indefinite and compares two objects, e.g.,

?areet ktaab ?aS^c^ab min ktaabak.

sakant fi beet ?akbar min haada lbeet.

min may show up either on the surface level as it is the case in the above examples or be represented as a gap that can be explained by the context in which it occurs, e.g.,

ktaabi ?ajdad (min ...) ?

miin ?akbar (beeti willa beetak, sayyaarti willa sayyaartak, ?abuuy willa ?abuuk, etc.) ?

The form conveys the superlative meaning when it is definite, e.g.,

haada ?aTwal walad fi SSaf.

haada ?akbar ši ^c^indi.

There are three forms of the elative in this dialect: ?aCCaC, ?aCaCC, and ?aCCa, where C stands for a consonant. ?aCCaC is derived from a base adjective that has three consonants where no two of the consonants are identical, e.g., *kbiir, Sa^{c}ib, sihil, rxiiS*. ?aCaCC is derived from a base form where the last two consonants are identical, e.g., *^{c}aziiz, SaHiiH, xafiif, šaHiiH*. ?aCCa is derived from base forms that have two consonants, e.g., *ɣaali, zaaki, haadi, Hilu*.

tamriin 6

Decide whether each adjectives in the following sentences is comparative or superlative. Give the reason(s) for your answer.

1. haadi ?akbar Taawla fi SSaff.
2. haadi lkursi ?akbar kursi fi beetna.
3. ljaww hoon ?abrad min ljaww fi Washington, D. C. fi ššita.
4. ljaww hoon ?abrad ši.
5. beetna ?akbar beet fi ššaari^{c}.
6. sayyaarit Hseen ?ajdad sayyaara hoon.
7. sayyaarit hišaam ?ajdad min sayyaarti.
8. l^{c}arabi ?aS^{c}ab luɣa fi l^{c}aalam.
9. l?isbaani ?ashal min SSiini.
10. ?iiTaalya ?aHsan min biriiTaanya.

tamriin 7

Construct six sentences from the following table.

			London
	?akbar		?ooroobba
?ustaazna	?ajmal madiina		Dallas
lluɣa l^{c}arabiyya	?a?wa		?ustaazkum
Ohio State	?aS^{c}ab luɣa	min	ljaam^{c}a
Chicago	?aHsan		Bush
Gorbachev	?aHsan jaam^{c}a	fi	Ohio
baariis	?azka		lluɣa lfaransiyya
	?ashal		lluɣa rruusiyya

tamriin 8

Complete the following sentences. Some sentences allow for comparative meaning only, some allow for superlative meaning, and some allow for both.

1. nahr nniil ?aTwal nahir .... .
2. lqaahira ?akbar min .... .
3. štareet ?aHsan sayyaara .... .
4. štareet banTaloon ?aHsan .... .
5. jamaal ?a?Sar .... .
6. sakanna fi ?akbar .... .
7. baskun fi ɣurfa ?azɣar .... .
8. zurt ?a?dam .... .

Listen toTape Segment #22

fi lbank l^{c}arabi b^{c}ammaan

zzbuuna: marHaba!
limHaasib: ?ahleen, ?ayy xidma ya ?uxt ?
zzbuuna: biddi ?aftaH Hsaab fi lbank.
limHaasib: šu noo^c liHsaab ?illi biddik tiftaHii ?
zzbuuna: kam noo^c min liHsaab ^{c}indkum ?
limHaasib: ^{c}indna noo^{c}een: Hsaab jaari wHsaab tawfiir. ^{c}ašaan tiftaHi Hsaab tawfiir laazim tHuTTi xamis miit diinaar ^{c}ala l?a?al.
zzbuuna: Tayyib, xalliini ?aftaH Hsaab jaari ?izan. hadool 250 dinaar.
limHaasib: ?iHna bnidfa^c 3% mirbaH ^{c}ala liHsaab ljaari.
zzbuuna: bass ?
limHaasib: ?aywa, bass ?iza btiftaHi Hsaab tawfiir bnidfa^{c}lik 9%.
zzbuuna: Tayyib xalliini ?afakkir šwayy.
limHaasib: leeš la?. lamma bit?ariri ?itiSli fiyya.

* * * * * * *

maysuun: ?asalaamu ^{c}alaykum!
limHaasib: wa^{c}alaykum-i-ssalaam, ?ayy xidma ya ?uxt ?
maysuun: biddi ?aSruf ha ššek, min faDlak.
limHaasib: ma^{c}ik hawiyya ?aw jawaaz safar ?
maysuun: ma^{c}i hawiyya, tfaDDal.
limHaasib: šukran. mumkin twa?^{c}i ^{c}ala xalf ššek wtukutbi ttaariix, min faDlik ?
maysuun: (ba^{c}d ma wa??a^{c}at ššek) tfaDDal.
limHaasib: haada mablaɣ kbiir, biddik ?iyyaa jamii^{c}u kaaš willa biddik tHuTTi ?isim minnu fi Hsaabik ?
maysuun: biddi ?iyyaa kullu kaaš ?iza fiš ^{c}indak maani^c
limHaasib: la?, ma fiš ?ayy maani^c. tfaDDali, haadi lifluus.
maysuun: šukran.

* * * * * * *

sa^{c}iid: marHaba!
limwaZZaf: ?ahleen. šu btu?mur ya ?ax ?

sa^{c}iid: biddi ?asakkir Hsaabi fi banikkum.

limwaZZaf: xeer! šu l?uSSa ?

sa^{c}iid: biddi ?asaafir ^{c}ala lqaahira ^{c}ašaan ?adrus majisteer hunaak.

limwaZZaf: mabruuk. šu biddak tudrus hunaak ?

sa^{c}iid: ?alla ybaarik fiik. biddi ?adrus ?idaarit ?a^{c}maal.

limwaZZaf: ^{c}aZiim. ma^{c}ak hawiyya ?

sa^{c}iid: tfaDDal.

limwaZZaf: šukran. ?ilak ^{c}indna 476 dinaar w41 ?irš. tfaDDal, haadi fluusak.

sa^{c}iid: šukran.

limwaZZaf: mwaffa? fi diraastak!

sa^{c}iid: jam^{c}an.

lmufradaat

zbuun (pl. zabaayin)	customer
mHaasib (pl. mHaasbiin)	teller
mwaZZaf (pl. mwaZZafiin)	employee
fataH (baftaH)	to open
Hsaab	account
Hsaab jaari	checking account
Hsaab tawfiir	savings account
HaTT (baHuTT)	to deposit
^{c}ala l?a?al/?aliila	at least
mirbaH	interest
fakkar (bafakkir)	to think
?arar (ba?arir)	to decide

?itaSal (bataSil)	to contact
Saraf (baSruf)	to cash, to spend
wa??a^c (bawa??i^c)	to sign
mumkin	Is it possible?
xalf	back (of the check)
mablaγ	amount (of money)
jamii^c	all of
kaaš	cash
hawiyya	identity card
jawaaz safar	passport
?isim	part, portion
maani^c	objection
fiš ?ayy maani^c	there is no objection
sakkar (basakkir)	to close
?uSSa	story
šu l?uSSa ?	What's the matter?
^{c}aZiim	great
majisteer	master's (degree)
bakalooryos	bachelor of arts/science
duktooraa	doctorate
?idaarit ?a^{c}maal	business administration
diraasa (pl. diraasaat)	study

Other vocabulary found in the following exercises or on tape

msakkar	closed
saHab (basHab)	to withdraw
^{c}aamal (ba^{c}aamil)	to deal with
ya^{c}ni	meaning, that is, in other words
mamnuu^c	forbidden
Hawwal (baHawwil)	to transfer
lbank lmarkazi	central bank
ma^{c}naaha	in that case
kifaaya	enough
^{c}umuula	charge, commission
bil?iDaafa ?ilaa	in addition to

tamriin 1

jaawib ^{c}ala l?as?ila ttaaliya.

1. kam Hsaab fii fi lbank l^{c}arabi ?
2. ?addeeš lmirbaH ^{c}ala Hsaab ttawfiir w^{c}ala liHsaab ljaari ?
3. leeš raaHat maysuun ^{c}ala lbank ?
4. leeš raaH sa^{c}iid ^{c}ala lbank ?
5. leeš biddu ysakkir sa^{c}iid Hsaabu fi lbank l^{c}arabi ?
6. šu biddu yudrus fi lqaahira ?

tamriin 2

?ixtaar ljawaab SSaHiiH.

1. raaHat-i-zzbuuna ^{c}ala lbank ^{c}ašaan .... .
   - a. tiftaH Hsaan tawfiir   b. tiftaH Hsaab jaari
   - c. tiftaH Hsaab
2. ma fatHatiš zzbuuna Hsaab jaari li?annu .... .
   - a. kaan ma^{c}ha 250 dinaar bass
   - b. lmirbaH ^{c}ala liHsaab ljaari 3%
   - c. lmirbaH ^{c}ala liHsaab ljaari 9%
3. ^{c}ašaan yuSruf zbuun šekk fi lbank l^{c}arabi laazim ykuun ma^{c}u .... .
   - a. hawiyya ?aw jawaaz safar
   - b. hawiyya bass (bass means only in this context)
   - c. jawaaz safar bass (bass means only in this context)
4. sakkar sa^{c}iid Hsaabu fi lbank l^{c}arabi li?annu .... .
   - a. biddu ysaafir ^{c}ala maSir
   - b. biddu yiftaH Hsaab fi bank taani
   - c. biddu lifluus ^{c}ašaan yšimm lhawa
5. bnifham min lqiT^{c}a ?innu .... .
   - a. ?ilha maysuun Hsaab fi lbank l^{c}arabi
   - b. ma lhaaš maysuun Hsaab fi lbank l^{c}arabi
   - c. ?ilha Hsaab fi bank lqaahira
6. ?axdat maysuun lmablaɣ kullu kaaš li?annu .... .
   - a. lmablaɣ kbiir   b. Hsaabha fi lbank l^{c}arabi msakkar
   - c. bidha ?iyyaa kullu kaaš

6. biddu sa^{c}iid yudrus fi maSir .... .
   - a. muHaasaba   b. ?idaarit ?a^{c}maal
   - c. majisteer siyaasa

tamriin 3

?ixtaar ljawaab SSaHiiH (Review the vocabulary words and their uses carefully before you start this exercise.)

1. lamma btištri maysuun fustaan hiyye ... šekk.
   a. btuSruf b. btuktub
2. lamma btiftaH Hsaab fi lbank bitSiir ... .
   a. mwazzaf fi hadaak lbank b. zbuun la hadaak lbank
3. nnaas ^{c}aadatan ... mirbaH ^{c}ala fluushum fi lbank.
   a. byidfa^{c}u b. byaaxdu
4. ^{c}ašaan tiftaH Hsaab jaari laazim ... fluus fi lbank.
   a. tHuTT b. tuSruf
5. ... nnaas fluushim lamma bisakru Hsaabhum fi lbank.
   a. biHuTTu b. byisHabu
6. ?ustaaz ljaam^{c}a bikuun ^{c}aadatan ma^{c}u ... .
   a. bakalooryus b. duktooraa

tamriin 4

Match each item in column A with one item in column B.

A	B
1. fii fi lbank Hsaabeen	a. byit^{c}aamal ma^c lbank
2. bakalooryus ya^{c}ni	b. kaaš
3. mwazzaf	c. Hsaab ttawfiir
4. zbuun	d. dafa^{c}lu lbank 10% mirbaH
5. byuSruf John ššekk	e. fi lbank
6. bidha naadya lmablaγ kullu	f. diraasa ?arba^c sniin fi ljaam^{c}a
7. biddi ?aHuTT ?isim min ššekk fi	g. miit ?irš
8. lamma fataH ?aHmad Hsaab tawfiir	h. byištγil fi lbank
9. ^{c}ašaan yuSruf Hasan ššekk	i. laazim ywa??i^c ^{c}ala xalfu
10. dinaar ya^{c}ni	j. Hsaab tawfiir wHsaab jaari

tamriin 5

Complete the following sentences. (Note that verbs after *laazim* should be in the subjunctive mood)

1. ^{c}ašaan tuSruf ššekk laazim .... .
2. ^{c}ašaan tit^{c}allam ^{c}arabi mniiH laazim .... .
3. laazim yHuTT Brad ^{c}ala l?a?al ... ^{c}ašaan yidfa^{c} lbank 8% mirbaH.
4. laazim titSil fi l?ustaaz ?iza .... .
5. ?iza ma ^{c}indakiš ?ayy maani^{c} laazim .... .

Forming nouns from verbs in Arabic

One of the common noun categories in Arabic is verbal nouns. A verbal noun is a noun derived from a verb. For example, the noun *diraasa* meaning "studying" is derived from the verb *daras*. Verbal nouns are usually rendered into gerunds in English. There are many patterns of verbal nouns in Arabic. These patterns are usually grouped in Arabic linguistic literature according to their plural patterns, not singular ones. Drawing rules to predict which noun patterns derive from which verb patterns is often not straightforward. For example, verbal noun patterns derived form the first form of the verb (i.e., *fa^{c}al*) fall in more than ten patterns. Some patterns, however, are more predictable and more regular than others. At the moment the best way to learn the verbal patterns is to take them one by one as they come along without attempting to form rules. The following is a list of some of the verbs that have been introduced in this course and the verbal nouns derived from these verbs.

verb	verbal nouns	gloss
katab	kitaaba	writing
daras	diraasa	studying
sakan	sakan	living, residing
?akal	?akil	eating
dafa^{c}	daf^{c}	paying, payment
saafar	safar	traveling
šaaf	šoof	seeing
naam	noom	sleeping
zaar	ziyaara	visiting
wa??a^{c}	taw?ii^{c}	signing
fakkar	tafkiir	thinking
širib	šurb	drinking

li^{c}ib	lu^{c}b	playing
riji^c	rujuu^c	returning, coming back
^{c}imil	^{c}amal	doing
?aja	majii?	coming
?ara	?i?raaya	reading
t^{c}allam	ta^{c}allum	learning
tkallam	takallum	speaking
?itaSal	?itiSaal	contact

tamriin 6

Fill in the blanks with the appropriate verbal nouns from the list above. Keep in mind that verbal nouns are usually definite. A noun can be definite in Arabic in one of four cases: (1) when the definite article *?al-* is added to it; (2) when a pronoun is attached to it; (3) when it is part of a noun construct where the last part of it is definite; and (4) when it is a proper noun (a proper noun is always definite).

1. ... fi Ohio State Sa^{c}ba ktiir. (daras)
2. saami biHibbiš .... (?ara)
3. ... lHummuS miš Sa^{c}ib. (^{c}imil)
4. ?ana baHibb .... (naam)
5. ... lxamir mamnuu^c fi ssa^{c}uudiyya. (širib)
6. ... fi madiinat New York γaali ktiir. (sakan)
7. Jim byištri ^{c}aadatan ... ^{c}arabi. (?akal)
8. nnaas fi ?ameerka biHibbu ... ktiir. (saafar)

tamriin 7 (Homework)

Write a paragraph in Arabic in response to a letter you receive from a friend of yours asking about the best bank in your hometown. In this paragraph give as many details and as many reasons as possible to support your choice.

Listen to Tape Segment #23

fi ?uteel l?ambasadoor fi l?uds

yaasiin: haloo, maktab taksiyyaat ^{c}abdu[1].

Karen: haloo. ?ana saayHa ?ameerkaaniyya ?ismi Karen. ?ana halla fi ?uteel l?ambasadoor, ^{c}aawza taksi ^{c}ašaan yaaxudni ^{c}ala beet laHim.

yaasiin: ?eemta biddik ttaksi ?

Karen: ba^{c}id see^{c}a ta?riiban.

yaasiin: ?inti liwaHdik willa ma^{c}ik suyyaaH taanyiin ?

Karen: ?ana liwaHdi.

yaasiin: ^{c}ašaan ?inti liwaHdik, ?ujrit ttaksi raayHa tkuun ɣaalya šwayy.

Karen: ?addeeš raayHa tkuun ?

yaasiin: talaatiin duulaar ta?riiban.

Karen: miš muhim. badfa^{c} talaatiin duulaar.

yaasiin: Tayyib, fi ?ayy ɣurfa ?inti fi l?uteel ?

Karen: fi ɣurfa 710, bass raayHa ?astanna ^{c}ala madxal l?uteel ba^{c}id see^{c}a.

yaasiin: mumtaaz. raayiH ?ab^{c}atlik taksi ba^{c}id see^{c}a loonu ?aSfar wnoo^{c}u Mercedes. mniiH ?

Karen: mniiH. šukran.

---

[1]taksiyyaat ^{c}abdu is an actual local cab company that operates in the Old City of Jerusalem.

yaasiin: ^{c}afwan, ma^{c} ssalaama.

Karen: ?alla ysallmak.

* * * * *

Karen: haada ttaksi ?illi ba^{c}atu maktab taksiyyaat ^{c}abdu ?

ššufeer: ?aywa. ?inti Karen ?

Karen: na^{c}am ?ana Karen.

ššufeer: tšaraffna, tafaDDali, ?udxuli fi ssayyaara.

Karen: šukran. biddi ?aštri filim lalkamara min stuudyo lHamra ^{c}ala TTarii?, mumkin ?

ššufeer: tu?umri ya sitt Karen, ?ayy ši taani ?

Karen: salaamtak. ?addeeš btaaxud rriHla Hatta naSal beet laHim ?

ššufeer: nuSS ssee^{c}a ta?riiban.

Karen: twakkal ^{c}ala ?alla ?izan! xalliina nimši.

ššufeer: ya ?allaah!

* * * * *

fi madiinat beet laHim

Karen: ?addeeš l?ujra ya ?ax ?

ššufeer: sitta w^{c}išriin duulaar wnuSS.

Karen: tfaDDal haadool talaatiin duulaar. xalli lbaa?i ^{c}ašaanak.

ššufeer: šukran.

Karen: ^{c}afwan.

lmufradaat

yaasiin	a male name
saayiH/a (pl. suyyaaH)	tourist
ᶜaayiz	I need
beet laHim	Bethlehem
?ujra	charge, wage
miš muhim	It does not matter.
madxal (pl. madaaxil)	entrance
maxraj (pl. maxaarij)	exit
baᶜat (babᶜat)	to send
daxal (badxul)	to get into, to enter
Tarii? (pl. Turu?)	way, road
tu?umr/i/u, HaaDir	at your service
salaamtak	nothing but your comfort and safety
twakkal ᶜala llaah	go on, proceed (rely on God)
baa?i	the rest, change
ᶜašaanak/ik	for yourself (tipping)
šufeer (pl. šufariyya)	driver

Other vocabulary found in the following exercises or on tape

faatuura (pl. fawaatiir)	a bill
?ahil	family members (especially members of the extended family)
ᶜaamil (pl. ᶜummaal)	a worker
binaaya (pl. mabaani)	a building
radd (barudd)	to answer
baγšiiš	tipping
jalas (bajlis)	to sit down
malyaan	full
maftuuH	open
Hamal (baHmil)	to carry
Hurr	free
?ista?jar (basta?jir)	to rent
makaan	a place
mawjuud	available, exists
šakil (pl. ?aškaal)	shape
tarak (batruk)	to leave

balad (pl. blaad) — a town
daaxil — inside

tamriin 1

1. min ween Karen ?
2. šu bitsaawi fi l?uds ?
3. ween naazla fi l?uds ?
4. ^{c}a ween bidha truuH ?
5. ma^{c} ?ayy maktab taksiyyaat ?itaSlat ?
6. miin radd ^{c}aleeha ?
7. ?eemta raayiH yijiiha ttaksi ?
8. šu loon wnoo^{c} ttaksi ?
9. ween raayHa tistanna ttaksi ?
10. šu bidha tištri min TTarii? ?
11. min ween raayHa tištri lfilm ?
12. ?addeeš byaaxud ssafar min l?uds labeet laHim bittaksi ?
13. ?addeeš daf^{c}at Karen ?ujrit ttaksi ?
14. ?addeeš ?a^{c}Tat šufeer ttaksi baγšiiš ?

tamriin 2

?ixtaar ljawaab SSaHiiH.

1. Karen fi l?uds ^{c}ašaan .... .
   a. tšimm lhawa   b. tzuur ?ahilha
   c. tu^{cc}ud fi ?uteel l?ambasadoor
2. ?itaSlat Karen bmaktab taksiyyaat ^{c}abdu ...
   a. ^{c}ašaan yib^{c}atilha lmaktab taksi Mercedes ?aSfar
   b. li?anha bidha tištri filim min stoodyo lHamra
   c. li?anha bidha truuH ^{c}ala beet laHim
3. Karen raayHa tistanna ttaksi .... .
   a. fi γurfitha   b. ^{c}ala madxal l?uteel   c. fi γurfa 710
4. ?ujrit ttaksi min l?uds labeet laHim bitkallif .... .
   a. nuSS ssee^{c}a   b. talaatiin dulaar ta?riiban
   c. talat dulaaraat ta?riiban
5. stoodyo lHamra .... .
   a. ^{c}ala TTarii? been l?uds wbeet laHim
   b. fi l?uds
   c. fi beet laHim

6. ?ujrit ttaksi kaanat ɣaalya li?annu ... .
   a. Karen wa??afat ᶜala TTarii? ᶜašaan tištri film
   b. ttaksi kaan Mercedes
   c. Karen kaanat liwaHdha

tamriin 3

?ixtaar ljawaab SSaHiiH (Review the vocabulary words and their uses before you start answering the questions below.)

1. ... ᶜaadatan byinzil fi ?uteel wbišimm lhawa.
   a. l?ustaaz   b. ssaayiH
2. ?addeeš Talab minnak lᶜaamil ... ?
   a. ?ujra   b. dulaar
3. ?aᶜadt ?adawwir ᶜala ... libnaaya ?aktar min seeᶜa.
   a. mabna   b. madxal
4. ššufrajiyya byištiɣilu ᶜala ... bass.
   a. dulaareen fi sseeᶜa   b. lbaɣšiiš
5. širkit taksiyyaat Yellow Cab ᶜaawza ... ktiir.
   a. šufariyya   b. neersaat

Active participle and progressive action in this dialect

The imperfect form of the verb (e.g., *badrus, baskun, baktub, balᶜab*) tends to express the progressive as well as the habitual (simple present) action in this dialect. The context usually provides the intended interpretation of the verb. In some cases, however, the active participle form CaaCiC, where C stands for a consonant, is used to express the progressive action. Consider the following examples where the active particle is underlined.

1. ?ana <u>raayiH</u> ᶜala ljaamᶜa meaning "I am going to the university."
2. huwwe <u>naayim</u> meaning "He is sleeping."
3. humme <u>?aaᶜdiin</u> meaning "They are awake/sitting down."

Not all active participles in Arabic express a progressive act. Those participles derived from verbs of motion such as *raayiH, raajiᶜ, maaši,* and *jaay* and those derived from verbs denoting a state (of things) such as *naayim, saakin, ᶜaayiš,* and *?aayim* express a progressive act. Like English, participle derived from verbs of motion may be used to convey the meaning of near future, e.g.,

1. ?aHmad raayiH ᶜala ljaamᶜa bukra. meaning "Ahmad is going to the university tomorrow."

2. raaj^{c}a widaad min maSir ba^{c}id ?usbuu^{c}. meaning "Widad is coming back from Egypt after a week."

The remaining majority of active participles denote various specific meanings and functions that need not be learned at this stage.

Unlike regular verbs, participles have three forms only: a masculine singular (e.g., *raayiH*), a feminine singular (e.g., *raayHa*), and a plural form (e.g., *raayHiin*), and they are negated by *miš* instead of the expected verb negation markers.

The following is a list of the active participles that can be used to express a progressive or future act. The verbs from which these participles are derived are given on the left column.

Verb	present participle
baskun	saakin
ba^{cc}ud	?aa^{c}id
banaam	naayim
bajlis	jaalis
badxul	daaxil
baxruj	xaarij
barja^{c}	raaji^{c}
ba?uum	?aayim
baruuH	raayiH
bamši	maaši
baaji	jaay

tamriin 4

Change each of the verbs given below from a simple habitual act into a progressive one following the example given below. Other changes in the sentence may also be necessary.

Example: widaad bitruuH ^{c}ala ssuu? kull yoom sabt.
widaad raayiHa ^{c}ala ssuu? halla.

1. John byuskun fi beet zɣiir.
2. muSTafa byiiji ^{c}ala maktabu maši kull yoom.
3. ?iHna bnu^{cc}ud nitfarraj ^{c}ala ttilvizyoon see^{c}teen kull yoom.
4. xaalid byijlis janb sihaam fi SSaff.
5. hiyye btirja^{c}iš min lmadrasa ssee^{c}a waHada.

Verbs with two objects in this dialect

Some verbs in Arabic take two objects; one is a direct object and the other is indirect. In many cases the indirect object and the preposition that precedes it are attached to the verb. For example, when *yaasiin* says *raayiH ?ab^{c}atlik taksi ba^{c}id see^{c}a* the word *?ab^{c}atlik* can be segmented into *?ab^{c}at* "to send," *-l-* "to," and *-ik* "you in the accusative form." The common term used to denote pronouns like *-ik* is attached pronouns. Also, the verb taking the two objects always agrees with the subject of the sentence. Therefore, a word like *?ab^{c}atlik* is a complex word: it incorporates a subject-verb marker, a verb, a preposition, and an indirect object.

The following table shows some of the verbs that take two objects.

?ana humme huwwe hiyye ?iHna	ɣasal HaDDar ^{c}imil katab ba^{c}at	la	?inta humme ?intu hiyye huwwe ?inti	maktuub sayyaara dawa ?akil l?amiiS

tamriin 5

Form five sentences from the table above following the example below. Remember that pronouns change according to their position in the sentence.

Example: baɣsullak l?amiiS "I will/wash the shirt for you."

1. ....
2. ....
3. ....
4. ....
5. ....

tamriin 6

Fill in the blanks with the correct form of the verb from the following list.

dafa^c, daxal, ?a^{c}ad, kaan, ?axad, ba^{c}at, wiSil

1. kiif bitHibbi ... lfaatuura, kaaš willa šekk ?
2. l?ustaaz raayiH ... fi maktabu bukra.
3. ?addeeš ... rilHiltak min Chicago la Los Angeles ?
4. lamma ... kaan lmaT^{c}am malyaan zabaayin.
5. lamma taSal Londan, ... maktuub.
6. tfaDDal ... ya ^{c}ali, lbaab maftuuH.

tamriin 7 (Homework)

Construct a similar dialogue in which you call a Yellow Cab to take you to the airport tomorrow at 7:30 a.m. Be as creative as you can in constructing the dialogue.

Listen to Tape Segment #24

fi funduq ssalaam fi l^{c}aqaba

Jack: marHaba!

xaliil: ?ahleen, šu btu?mur ya ?ax ?

Jack: baffakir ?a^{cc}ud fi haada l?uteel muddit ?usbuu^c.

xaliil: ?ahlan wasahlan. ma^{c}ak Had willa liwaHdak ?

Jack: zoojti ma^{c}i.

xaliil: šu noo^c lγurfa ?illi biddak ?iyyaaha ?

Jack: kam noo^c min lγuraf ^{c}indkum ?

xaliil: ^{c}indna sitt ?anwaa^c. γuraf fiiha taxt mifrid, γuraf fiiha taxt mijwiz, γuraf fiiha taxteen mifrid, γuraf fiiha taxteen mijwiz, wγuraf fiiha taxteen mijwiz ma^c balkoona w^{c}indna kamaan Saala.

Jack: fii tilvizyoonaat wtalafoonaat fi lγuraf ?

xaliil: kull γurfa fiiha tilivzyoon mlawan wtalafoon wHammaam.

Jack: šu l?as^{c}aar ^{c}indkum ?

xaliil: ?arxaS ši SSaala, dinaareen fi lleela. ba^{c}deen lγurfa btaxt mifrid b?arba^c danaaniir, lγurfa btaxt mijwiz bsitt danaaniir, lγurfa btaxteen mifrid bsitt danaaniir kamaan, wilγurfa btaxteen mijwiz wbalkoona bsabi^c danaaniir. fii ^{c}inda kamaan birkit sbaaHa wara l?uteel, ssbaaHa fiiha blaaš.

Jack: ^{c}aZiim. ^{c}indkum baar wmaT^{c}am ?

xaliil: ^{c}inda maT^{c}am bass ma ^{c}indnaaš baar. bti^{c}raf haada balad ?islaami wiššurb fii mamnuu^c.

Jack: Tayyib. l?akil maHsuub ma^c ?ujrit l?uteel ?

xaliil: la?. btidfa^{c}lu liwaHdu.

Jack: kiif si^{c}ir l?akil ?

xaliil: bitwa??af ^{c}ala noo^{c}u. ba^{c}D l?anwaa^c γaalya waba^{c}Dha rxiiSa.

Jack: Tayyib. ?a^{c}Tiini γurfa fiiha taxteen mijwiz ma^c balkoona.

xaliil: ma^{c}ak hawiyya ?aw jawaaz safar ?

Jack: ma^{c}i jawaaz safar.

xaliil: mumtaaz. ^{c}abbi ha TTalab wa?a^{c}Tiini ?iyyaa ma^c ljawaaz ^{c}ašaan ?a^{c}Tiik lmuftaaH.

lmufradaat

funduq (pl. fanaadiq)	hotel
salaam	peace
?ahlan wasahlan	welcome
Had (?aHad/waaHad)	someone
taxt mifrid	twin bed
taxt mijwiz	double bed
balkoona	balcony
Saala	a hall in a hotel used for several people to sleep in, a dorm
mlawan	colored
Hammaam	bathroom
blaaš	free
Hasab/maHsuub	to count/included
bitwa??af ^{c}ala	it depends on
^{c}abba (ba^{c}abbi)	to fill out
Talab	application

Other vocabulary found in the following exercises or on tape

muriiH	comfortable
tna??al (batna??al)	to move around
sbaaHa	swimming
janaaH (?ajniHa)	a suite in a hotel
takyiif	air-conditioning
malyaan	full
Hajaz (baHjiz)	to reserve, to book
Hajz	reservation
kart visa	Visa card
xaSim	discount
mazbuuT	right, correct

tamriin 1

1. ween Jack ?
2. šu byištγil xaliil ?
3. kam yoom biddu Jack yu^{cc}ud fi funduq ssalaam ?
4. kam noo^{c} min lγuraf fii fi funduq ssalaam ? šu humme ?
5. ?addeeš si^{c}ir kul γurfa ?
6. šu fii fi l?uteel kamaan ?
7. ?addeeš byidfa^{c} Jack ^{c}ašaan yisbaH fi birkit l?uteel ?
8. kiif ?as^{c}aar l?akil fi l?uteel ?
9. šu laazim yi^{c}mal Jack ^{c}ašaan yaaxud lmuftaaH ?
10. šu noo^{c} lγurfa ?illi raayiH yu^{cc}ud fiiha Jack wzoojtu ?

tamriin 2

?ixtaar ljawaab SSaHiiH.

1. Jack biddu yinzil fi ?uteel ssalaam lamuddit ... .

   a. sabi^{c} ?ayyaam b. xamis ?ayyaam c. ^{c}ašar ?ayyaam
2. fii fi findu? ssalaam ... .

   a. birkit sbaaHa wbaar b. birkit sbaaHa wmaT^{c}am.

   c. maT^{c}am wbaar
3. Jack kaan fi l^{c}aqaba ... .

   a. liwaHdu b. ma^{c} ?ibnu wzoojtu

   c. ma^{c} zoojtu bass
4. ššurb fi funduq ssalaam mamnuu^{c} li?annu ... .

   a. fiš fi lfunduq baar b. findu? Zγiir

   c. lkuHuul γaalya ktiir
5. ^{c}ašaan tinzil fi ?uteel fi l^{c}aqaba laazim ... .

   a. t^{c}abbi Talab wykuun ma^{c}ak jawaaz safar

   b. ykuun ma^{c}ak jawaaz safar bass

   c. ta^{c}abbi Talab bass
6. bnifham min lqiT^{c}a ?innu ?uteel ssalaam ... .

   a. kbiir b. zγiir c. zγiir ktiir

tamriin 3

?ixtaar ljawaab SSaHiiH (Review the vocabulary words and their uses before you start this exercise.)

1. ttaxt lmijwiz ^{c}aadatan ... min lmifrid.

   a. ?akbar b. ?azγar

2. ?addeeš si^{c}ir lγurfa fi ... fi haada l?uteel ?

   a. lyoom   b. lleela

3. l?akil miš ... ma^c si^{c}ir lγurfa.

   a. maHsuub   b. mamnuu^c

4. ^{c}ašaan tudxul ljaam^{c}a laazim t^{c}abbi .... .

   a. Taalib   b. Talab

5. ?iza btištri sayyaara jdiida ba^{c}Tuuk tilvizyoon .... .

   a. byištγilš   b.blaaš

6. šurb lkuHuul ... fi ?ameerka.

   a. masmuuH   b. mamnuu^c

tamriin 4

?i?ra lHiwaaraat ttaaliya wjaawib ^{c}ala l?as?ila taHthum.

1. A: kam yoom ?a^{c}adtu hunaak ?
   B: talat ?ayyaam.
   A: kiif kaanat lγuraf ?
   B: kaanat kbiira wmuriiHa wirxiiSa.
   A: kam taxt fii fi lγurfa ?
   B: taxteen mijwiz.
   su?aal: ween kaan naazil B ?

2. A: kiif raayiH titna??al fi ?isbaanya ya baasim ?
   baasim: bsayyaara sta?jaratha šširka.
   A: ?addeeš bitkalfak ssayyaara fi lyoom ?
   baasim: wala ši. šširka btidfa^c kull ttakaaliif.
   su?aal: ?addeeš raayH yidfa^c baasim takaaliif ssayyaara ?

3. A: ween btisbaH ya haani ?
   haani: fi birkit sbaaHit ?uteel lHoly Land.
   A: ?addeeš bitkallif ssbaaHa hunaak ?
   haani: blaaš.
   su?aal: ?addeeš byidfa^c haani ^{c}ašaan yisbaH fi birkit ?uteel lHoly Land ?

4. A: ?addeeš ?as^{c}aar lγuraf fi ?uteel hind ?
   B: bitwa??af ^{c}ala noo^c lγurfa.
   A: ?addeeš ?arxaS γurfa ?

B: talaatiin dulaar fi lleela.

su?aal: kiif ?as^{c}aar lɣuraf fi ?uteel hind ?

tamriin 5

Fill in the blanks with the correct form of the verb from the following list:

^{c}abba, dafa^{c}, fakkar, daxal, ba^{c}at, ?itaSal

1. ?eemta raayiH ... lmaktuub ya xaalid ?
2. ?addeeš ... Jim ?ujrit lbaaS lamma byiiji ^{c}ala ljaam^{c}a ?
3. ... Rick yoom ssabt lmaaDi biDebbie bass ma kaanatiš fi lbeet.
4. ?eemta ... miryam lɣurfa ?
5. ?iza biddak tsakkir Hsaabak fi lbank, xud haada TTalab w ... !

tamriin 6

Fill in the blanks in the following table with the correct form of the verbs.

Pronoun	Perfect	Indicative	Subjunctive	Imperative
?ana	dafa^{c}t			
?inta		btib^{c}at		
?inti				?uxruji
huwwe			yudxul	
hiyye	?itaSlat			
?iHna	^{c}abbeena			
?intu				^{c}abbu
humme		bifakru		

tamriin 7

An Arab friend of yours is coming to spend a weekend in your hometown. He writes asking you about a hotel or a motel where he could stay. Write a one-page description of a hotel you would recommend to your friend. In your description include information on the various facilities the hotel provides, the price, its location, the type of rooms, the size of the hotel, the hotel restaurant, and so on.

Listen to Tape Segment #25

fi maktab lbariid fi l?uds

kariim: marHaba!

lmuwaZZaf: ?ahleen, šu btu?mur ya ?ax ?

kariim: biddi ?ab^{c}at maktuub ^{c}ala faransa wTard ^{c}ala maSir.

lmuwaZZaf: kiif biddak tib^{c}athum, bilbariid l^{c}aadi willa ljawwi willa lbaHri?

kariim: šu raayak ? kiif btinSaHni ?ab^{c}athum ?

lmuwaZZaf: haada bitwa??af ^{c}ala ^{c}iddit ?ašyaa?. nnaas ^{c}aadatan byib^{c}atu lmakatiib bilbariid ljawwi wiTruud bilbariid lbaHri.

kariim: šu lfar? been lbariid ljawwi wilbaHri ?

lmuwaZZaf: lbariid ljawwi γaali bass sarii^{c}, lbariid lbaHri baTii? bass rxiiS.

kariim: ?addeeš btaaxud irrisaala Hatta taSal faransa bilbariid ljawwi ?

lmuwaZZaf: btaaxud ^{c}aadatan ?usbuu^{c}.

kariim: w?addeeš byaaxud TTard Hatta yaSal maSir bilbariid lbaHri ?

lmuwaZZaf: byaaxud ^{c}aadatan ?arba^{c} ?asaabii^{c}.

kariim: walaaw. haada byaaxud wa?t ktiir. ?izan, laazim ?ab^{c}athum bilbariid ljawwi, bass biddi ?ab^{c}at lmaktuub bilbariid limsajjal kamaan.

lmuwaZZaf: zayy maa biddak. lmaktuub bikallif tis^{c}iin ?irš wiTTard bikallif dinaar wrubu^{c}. btu?mur ?ayy ši taani ?

kariim: ?aywa, biddi kamaan ^{c}ašar Tawaabi^{c} maHalliyya wtalat Tawaabi^{c} ?iimit kull Taabic xamsa w^{c}išriin ?irš.[1]

---

[1]Note that speakers of Arabic identify overseas stamps by their value not by name. Each ?irš is worth approximately three cents. Thus, a stamp for twenty-five ?irš is equal to a seventy-five-cent stamp in the United States.

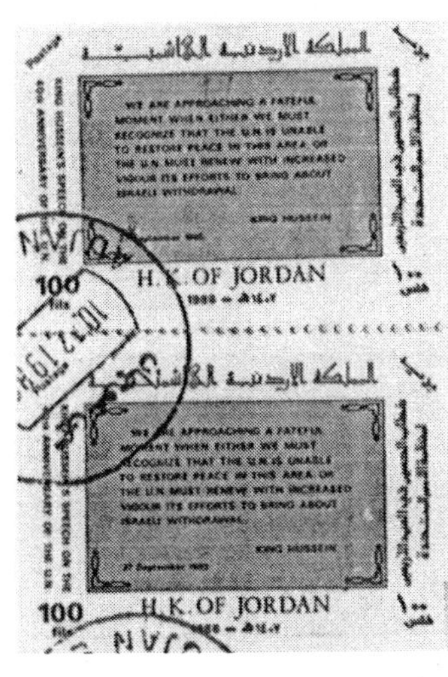

lmwaZZaf: tfaDDal. hadool bikalfu talat danaaniir wtis^{c}iin ?irš.
kariim: tfaDDal haadi war?at xamis danaaniir.
lmuwaZZaf: Tayyib. tfaDDal haadool dinaar w^{c}ašr ?i?ruuš lbaa?i.
kariim: mumkin tfikli ddinaar balla ? biddi ?ataSil mukaalama tilifooniyya min hoon.
lmuwaZZaf: btiHtajiš fakka ^{c}ašaan tista^{c}mil ttalafoon. btiHtaaj sammunaat.
kariim: min ween baštriihum ?
lmuwaZZaf: min hoon. bitkallif ssammuuna ?arb^{c}iin ?irš wmudditha talat da?aayi? lilmukaalama lmaHalliyya.
kariim: kam sammuuna biddi ^{c}ašaan ?ataSil bnaablis ?
lmuwaZZaf: biddak sammuuna lakull d?ii?a wnuSS.
kariim: Tayyib ?a^{c}Tiini sammuunteen ?izan.
lmuwaZZaf: tfaDDal.
kariim: šukran.

lmufradaat

maktab lbariid	post office
Tard	package, parcel
bariid ^{c}aadi	regular mail
bariid jawwi	airmail
bariid baHri	sea mail
naSaH (banSaH)	to advise, to recommend
^{c}idda	several
?ašyaa? (pl. of ši)	things/factors in this context

sarii^c	fast, express (mail)
baTii?	slow
walaaw	expression of surprise
msajjal	registered
bariid msajjal	registered mail
zayy maa biddak	as you wish
Taabi^c (pl. Tawaabi^c)	stamp
maHalli	local
?iima	value, price in this context
war?at xamis danaaniir	five-dinar bill
fakk (bafukk)	to break (i.e., a dollar into change), to change
fakka	change
mukaalama tilifooniyya	telephone call
?iHtaaj (baHtaaj)	to need
?ista^{c}mal (basta^{c}mil)	to use
sammuuna (Pl. sammuunaat)	telephone token

Other vocabulary found in the following exercises or tape

niZaam	system
xaariji	overseas
muna	Arabic female name
šahaadit milaad	birth certificate
Daa^c (baDii^c)	to get lost
wajad (balaa?i)	to find (a place closed)
maHaTTit baaSaat	bus station
talafoon ^{c}umuumi	public phone
maktaba (pl. maktabaat)	book store
faatuura (pl. fawaatiir)	a bill
fataH (baftaH)	to open
Sinf (pl. ?aSnaaf)	type, class
?istama^c (ba?astami^c)	to listen
^{c}ibaara (pl. ^{c}ibaaraat)	utterance, statement
jayyidan	carefully
?istahlak (ba?astahlik)	to consume
xuSuuSi	private
sayyid (pl. saada)	mister, sir
balad (pl. blaad)	country

baqqaala (pl. baqqaalaat)	grocery store
maahir	Arabic male name
baa^{c} (babii^{c})	to sell
baayi^{c}/bayyaa^{c} (pl. bayya^{c}iin)	a salesman
Zarf (pl. Zruuf)	an envelope
Tawwal (baTawwil)	to take a long time
badri	early
minTa?a	area

tamriin 1

1. leeš raaH kariim ^{c}ala maktab lbariid ?
2. šu ?anwaa^{c} lbariid lmawjuuda fi l?uds ?
3. šu biddu yib^{c}at kariim ^{c}ala faransa ? kiif biddu yib^{c}atu ?
4. ^{c}ala ween biddu yib^{c}at TTard ?
5. šu lfar? been lbariid ljawwi wilbariid lbaHri ?
6. kiif ?arrar kariim yib^{c}at lmaktuub wiTTard ?
7. b?ayy bariid byib^{c}atu nnaas ^{c}aadatan TTruud ?
8. ?addeeš si^{c}ir TTaabi^{c} lmaHalli ?
9. šu byista^{c}imlu nnaas fi l?uds ^{c}ašaan yitkallamu ^{c}ala talafoon ^{c}umuumi ?
10. ?addeeš si^{c}ir ssammuuna ?
11. fii sammuunaat talafoon fi ?ameerka ? šu byista^{c}imlu nnaas fi ?ameerka ^{c}ašaan yista^{c}imlu talafoon ^{c}umuumi ?

tamriin 2

?ixtaar ljawaab SSaHiiH.

1. raaH kariim ^{c}ala maktab lbariid ^{c}ašaan .... .
   a. yib^{c}at maktuub ^{c}ala faransa wTarD ^{c}ala maSir
   b. yištri Tawaabi^{c} wsammunaat
   c. a and b.
2. kallaf lmaktuub ^{c}ala faransa .... .
   a. xamsa w^{c}išriin ?irš b. tis^{c}iin ?irš c. dinaar wrubu^{c}
3. byaaxud TTard Hatta yaSal maSir bilbariid lbaHri .... .
   a. šahar b. ?usbuu^{c} waaHad c. sabi^{c} ?ayyaam
4. ^{c}ašaan tista^{c}mil talafoon ^{c}umuumi fi l?uds btiHtaaj .... .
   a. fakka b. sammuuna c. fakka wsammuuna

5. bitkallif lmukaalama ttalafooniyya lmaHalliyya limuddit sitt da?aayi? fi l?uds ... .
   a. sammuunteen   b. sittin ?irš   c. tamaaniin ?irš
6. ?iimit TTaabi^c lmaHalli fi l?uds ... .
   a. ^{c}ašar ?iruuš   b. tis^{c}iin ?irš   c. xamsa w^{c}išriin ?irš
7. lbariid lbaHri ... min lbariid ljawwi.
   a. ?aɣla   b. ?arxaS   c. ?asra^c
8. ba^{c}at kariim TTard bilbariid ... .
   a. ljawwi   b. lbaHri   c. limsajjal
9. kariim raayiH yitkallam ma^c naablus ... .
   a. ?arba^c da?aayi?   b. sitt da?aayi?   c. talat da?aayi?
10. bnifham min lqiT^{c}a ?innu niZaam lbariid fi l?uds ... .
   a. mitil niZaam lbariid fi baladna ta?riiban
   b. byixtilf ktiir ^{c}an niZaam lbariid fi baladna
   c. mniiH ktiir

tamriin 3

?ixtaar ljawaab SSaHiiH (Review the vocabulary words and their uses before you you begin this exercise.)

1. ^{c}ašaan tib^{c}at maktuub laazim tista^{c}mil ... .
   a. sammuunaat   b. Tawaabi^c
2. lbariid lbaHri ?arxaS w ... min lbariid ljawwi.
   a. ?asra^c b. ?abTa?
3. ^{c}ašaan yitSil Mark biNew York laazim ... ttalafoon.
   a. yista?jir   b. yista^{c}mil
4. ^{c}ašaan tib^{c}at maktuub min Boston ^{c}ala Atlanta laazim tista^{c}mil Taabi^c ... .
   a. maHalli   b. dawli
5. lmaktuub bilbariid ljawwi byaaxud wa?it ... min lbariid lbaHri.
   a. ?a?al   b. ?aktar
6. ^{c}ašaan tib^{c}at muna risaala min l?uds ^{c}ala London ... Taabi^c dawli.
   a. bitkallif   b. btiHtaaj
7. hadool dinaareen. ?a^{c}Tiini Tawaabi^c bdiinaar wi^{c}išriin ?irš w ... sammunaat.
   a. ?iimit   b. lbaa?i
8. ^{c}ašaan tistam^{c}il talafoon ^{c}ummuumi fi ?ameerka btiHtaaj ... .
   a. fakka   b. sammunaat

tamriin 4

?i?ra lHiwaaraat ttaaliya wjaawib ^{c}ala l?as?ila taHthum.

1. A: ?addeeš byaaxud haada lmaktuub Hatta yaSal Tokyo ?
   (The speaker is in Washington, D. C.)
   B: ?usbuu^{c} ta?riiban.
   A: mumtaaz. ?aTiini TTawaabi^{c} min faDlak!
   su?aal: fi ?ayy bariid ba^{c}at A lmaktuub ?

2. A: biddi ?ab^{c}at ha TTard ^{c}ala Colombia.
   B: kiif biddak tib^{c}atu ?
   A: ?arxaS ši.
   su?aal: fi ?ayy bariid ba^{c}at A TTard ?

3. A: fii fi haada lmaktuub šahaadit milaad wbiddiiš tDii^{c} bilbariid.
   B: ?ib^{c}atha bilbariid limsajjal ?izan.
   A: ?addeeš bitkallif rrisaala bilbariid limsajjal ?
   B: xamis dularaat.
   A: tfaDDal hadool xamis dularaat.
   su?aal: leeš ba^{c}at A lmaktuub bilbariid limsajjal ?

4. A: ruHt ^{c}ala maktab lbariid wwajadtu msakkir. ween bibii^{c}u Tawaabi^{c} hoon ?
   B: fi lmaktabaat, bass ssee^{c}a tamaanya halla wkull lmaktabaat msakra.
   su?aal: štara A Tawaabi^{c} ?

5. A: ween ?a?rab talafoon ^{c}umuumi hoon ?
   B: fi maHaTTit lbaaSaat. ?imši duγri fi haada ššaari^{c} Hawaali
   nuSS keelumitir. maHaTTit lbaaSaat bitkuun ^{c}ala ?iidak lyamiin.
   A: šukran ktiir.
   B: ^{c}afwan
   su?aal: leeš biddu yruuH A ^{c}ala maHaTTit lbaaSaat ?

tamriin 5

Provide the correct form of the verb given in parentheses in each of the following sentences.

1. bti?dar ... ha ddiinaar ya ?ax ? (fakk)

2. ?iza biddik ... ttalafoon laazim tištri sammuunaat. (?ista^{c}mal)
3. xaalid raaH ^{c}ala maktab lbariid w ... risaalteen ^{c}ala lyaabaan. (ba^{c}at)
4. Haawalu ... ma^{c} Sadii?hum ^{c}ali, bass ma kanš fi lbeet. (?itaSal)
5. Mary ... halla xamis miit dulaar ^{c}ašaan tidfa^{c} faatuurat lmustašfa. (?iHtaaj)

tamriin 6

Fill in the blanks.

1. ?a^{c}Tiini sammuunteen ^{c}ašaan ... .
2. byaaxud TTard Hatta yaSal lmaɣrib ... .
3. bikallif TTaabi^{c} lmaHalli ... .
4. bti?darš tištri Tawaabi^{c} min ... .
5. ?itaSil ma^{c}i talafoon lamma ... .
6. lbariid lmaHalli fi ?ameerka ?arba^{c} ?aSnaaf/darajaat, humme ... .

tamriin 7

Match the following two columns.

1. ba^{c}at rrisaala ^{c}ala rooma	a. ^{c}ašar ?iruuš
2. lbariid lbaHari ^{c}aadatan	b. sammuuna
3. ?iimit kull Taabi^{c}	c. Taabi^{c} bnuSS dulaar
4. miin ... ttalafoon l^{c}umuumi ?	d. zayy maa biddik
5. biddi ... ^{c}ašaan ?atSil ma^{c} Ken	e. maktab lbariid
6. rrisaala ^{c}ala Moscow btiHtaaj	f. bilbariid ljawwi
7. niZaam lbariid fi faransa	g. byista^{c}mil
8. ba^{c}at ššekk bilbariid	h. miš sarii^{c}
9. ?i^{c}mali	i. mniiH ktiir
10. byiftaH ... ssee^{c}a tamaanya SSubH	j. limsajjal

tamriin 8

Fill in the blanks with the correct forms of the verbs

Pronoun	Perfect	Indicative	Subjunctive	Imperative
?ana				
?inta				
?inti				
huwwe	?ista^{c}mal			
hiyye				
?iHna				
?intu				
humme				

?ana	fakkeet			
?inta				
?inti				
huwwe				
hiyye				
?iHna				
?intu				
humme				

?ana				
?inta				
?inti				
huwwe				
hiyye			tistami^{c}	
?iHna				
?intu				
humme				

tamriin 9

Write a one-page description of the postal system in your country. Use a dictionary for additional vocabulary if you need to.

Listen to Tape Segment #26

γassaan biddu yištri beet fi ^{c}ammaan

jamaal: MarHaba ya γassaan. weenak ? ?ilna zamaan ma šufnaak.

γassaan: kunt fi ?abu Dabi. Saarli baštγil hunaak talt sniin.

jamaal: ?ahlan wasahlan. ?addeeš saarlak hoon ?

γassaan: ?usbuu^{c} bass.

jamaal: šu raayiH ti?mal halla ?

γassaan: badeet ?adawwir ^{c}ala beet ^{c}ašaan ?aštrii.

jamaal: miš muškila. fii byuut ktiira ma^{c}ruuDa lalbee^{c}. šu Hajm lbeet ?illi biddak ?iyyaa.

γassaan: biddi beet zγiir fii γurufteen noom wγurfit juluus wimTbax wHimmaam.

γurfit juluus　　γurfit noom　　Hammaam

jamaal: biddak ?iyyaa Taabi? willa Taab?een.

γassaan: Taab?een bikuun ?aHsan.

jamaal: fi ^{c}ind jiraana beet mumtaaz. fii talat γuraf noom wγurfit juluus kbiira wHimmaameen wmiTbax wγurfit Sufra wgaraaj wHadii?a zγiira ?uddam lbeet. w?aHsan min heek, si^{c}ru miš baTTaal.

γassaan: ?addeeš bidhum fii ?

jamaal: Hawaali 25.000 diinaar, wbijuuz yinzalu la Had 20.000.

γassaan: balla!

jamaal: walla. bass fiš fi lbeet tadfi?a wala takyiif.

γassaan: lbeet Hajar willa baToon ?

jamaal: Hajar min talat jihaat wbaToon min jiha.

γassaan: lHadii?a kbiira ?

jamaal: ya^{c}ni, Hawaali miiteen mitir mrabba^{c}.

γassaan: ?eemta bni?dar nšuufu ?

jamaal: šu raayak tmurr ^{c}alay bukra ba^{c}d DDuhur. baruuH ?ana wiyyaak ^{c}aleehum ^{c}ašaan tšuufu.

γassaan: mumtaaz. ?ana bukra faaDi ba^{c}id ssee^{c}a tinteen. ween saakin ?inta ?

jamaal: fi šaari^{c} ?abu nuwaas, ra?am 221.

γassaan: bamurr ^{c}aleek bukra ssee^{c}a ?arba^{c}a ta?riiban.

jamaal: ?ahlan wasahlan.

γassaan: ?ibak.

lmufradaat

zamaan	long ago
ma^{c}ruuD	displayed (for)
bee^{c}	sale
ma^{c}ruuD lalbee^{c}	for sale
Hajm	size
γurfit noom	bedroom
γurfit juluus	living room
miTbax (pl. maTaabix)	kitchen
γurfit Sufra	dining room
Taabi? (pl. Tawaabi?)	floor
jaar/jiraan	neighbor
garaaj (pl. garaajaat)	a garage
Hadii?a (pl. Hadaayi?)	yard (garden)
tadfi?a	heating

takyiif (hawaa?i)	air-conditioning
mrabba^{c}	square
Hajar	stone
baToon	concrete
marr	to stop by
?iyyaak	you (objective case)
faaDi	free
?ibak/-ik/-kum	no problem (welcome to you, too)

Other vocabulary found in the following exercises or tape

waSSaf (bawaSSif)	to describe
faxim	magnificent
dirham	a monetary unit used in some parts of the Arab world
mka^{cc}ab	cubic
riyaaD	Arabic male name
salwa	Arabic female name
yabdu	it seems
mawqi^{c} (pl. mawaaqi^{c})	location
mnaasib	convenient
mabni	built, constructed
raaDi	satisfied, content
bitta?siiT	through financing
Tabii^{c}a	nature
Hanaan	Arabic female name
xaTT	script
Taba^{c} (baTba^{c})	to type
samaH (basmaH)	to permit
xadiija	Arabic female name
masaaHa	area
DaaHiya (pl. DawaaHi)	suburb
?ista^{c}mal (basta^{c}mil)	to use
maktab	a desk
^{c}aadil	Arabic male name
rašiid	Arabic female name
?ista?jar (basta?jir)	to rent (a house for yourself)
?ajjar (ba?ajjir)	to rent (your house to someone)

bidaaya	beginning
haadi	quiet
tzawwaj (batzawwaj)	to get married
salafan	in advance

tamriin 1

jaawib ^{c}ala l?as?ila ttaaliya.

1. šu biddu yi^{c}mal γassaan fi ^{c}ammaan ?
2. ween kaan γassaan ?
3. ?addeeš Saarlu hunaak ?
4. ?eemta riji^{c} ^{c}ala ^{c}ammaan ?
5. ?addeeš Hajm lbeet ?illi biddu yištrii ?
6. miin biddu ybii^{c} beetu ?
7. ?addeeš bidhum fii ?
8. waSSif lbeet ?
9. ?eemta raayiH γassaan yšuuf lbeet ?
10. ween byuskun jamaal ?

tamriin 2

?ixtaar ljawaab SSaHiiH.

1. γassaan Saarlu byištγil fi ?abu Dabi .... .
   a. talt sniin b. xams sniin c. ^{c}ašar sniin
2. bnifham min lqiT^{c}a ?innu .... .
   a. γassaan ma^{c}u fluus tkaffi beet
   b. γassaan ma^{c}iš fluus min marra
   c. γassaan γani ktiir ktiir
3. biddu γassaan yištri beet .... .
   a. kbiir b. zγiir c. faxim
4. biHubb γassaan beetu ykuun .... .
   a. Taabi? waaHad b. Taab?een c. ?aktar min Taab?een
5. ... bidhum ybii^{c}u beethum.
   a. jamaal b. jiraam γassan c. jiraan jamaal
6. bidhum jiraan jamaal fi beethum .... .
   a. ^{c}išriin ?alf diinaar b. xamsa w^{c}išriin ?alf diinaar
   c. xamsa wi^{c}išriin dirham
7. lbeet maSnuu^{c} min .... .
   a. lbaToon b. lHajar c. lbaToon wilHajar

8. fii fi lbeet ... .

   a. tadfi?a   b. birkit sbaaHa   c. Hadii?a zγiira

9. jamaal byuskun fi ... .

   a. šaari^{c} ^{c}ammaan   b. šaari^{c} γassaan   c. šaari^{c} ?abu nuwaas

10. ra?am beet jamaal ... .

   a. 25,000   b. 20,000   c. 221

tamriin 3

?ixtaar ljawaab SSaHiiH.

1. ma ruHtiš ^{c}ala ssinama min ... .

   a. zamaan   b. Taab?een

2. fi ššita nnaas byista^{c}imlu ... .

   a. ttakyiif   b. ttadfi?a

3. šu raayak ... ^{c}ala maktab ddaktoor saliim witsallim ^{c}alee ?

   a. twa??if   b. tmurr

4. ... ^{c}indhum Hadii?a kbiira

   a. beethum   b. jiraanna

5. masaaHit beeti 220 mitir ... .

   a. mrabba^{c} b. mka^{cc}ab

6. byista^{c}imlu nnaas fi byuuthum ... fi SSeef.

   a. ttakyiif   b. ssayyaara

7. nnaas ^{c}aadatan binaamu fi ... .

   a. γurfit ljuluus   b. γurfit nnoom

8. l?amerkaan byitfarraju ^{c}aadatan ^{c}ala ttilvizyoon fi ... .

   a. lHimmaam   b. γurfit ljuluus

9. raayiH ?asaafir ^{c}ala California ššahar ljaay. ^{c}ašaan heek biddi ... beeti fi New York.

   a. ?abii^{c} b. ?aštri

10. biddu riyaaD yištri ... btalat Twaabi?.

   a. Hadii?a   b. beet

tamriin 4

?i?ra lHiwaaraat ttaaliya wjaawib ^{c}ala l?as?ila taHthum.

1. A: biddi ?abii^{c} beeti w?aštri beet ?akbar ya salwa.

   salwa: xeer, beetak mniiH wijdiid ?

   A: tzawwajt ?abil sana w?ajaani walad zγiir.

   salwa: mabruuk! ma ti?la?š fii byuut ktiir ma^{c}ruuDa lalbee^{c}.

su?aal: leeš biddu A yištri beet ?

2. A: ?eemta štareet beetak ya maHmuud ?
maHmuud: ?abil taman sniin.
A: ?addeeš kaan tamanu ?
maHmuud: talaatiin ?alf dulaar.
A: haada si^{c}ir miš baTTaal.
maHmuud: heek kaanat ?as^{c}aar libyuut.
su?aal: miin ?arxaS libyuut halla willa ?abil taman sniin ? kiif ^{c}rift ?

3. A: ?addeeš Saarlak btuskun fi haada lbeet ?
B: xamis ta^{c}šar sana.
A: yabdu ?innu beet mniiH.
B: la?. bass mawqi^{c}u mnaasib w?ujurtu rxiiSa.
su?aal: bnifham min lHiwaar ?innu ... .
   a. B mabsuuT ktiir fi lbeet ?illi byuskun fii
   b. B miš mabsuuT min marra fi lbeet
   c. B raaDi fi lbeet li?annu si^{c}ru wmawqi^{c}u mnaasbiin

4. A: kam γurfa fii fi beetak ?
B: γurufteen noom wHammaam wγurfit juluus wmiTbax wbalkoona.
A: haada beet zγiir ktiir.
B: zγiir bass mumtaaz. fii tadfi?a wtakyiif wmabni kullu min lHajar.
su?aal: bnifham min lHiwaar ?innu ... .
   a. B mabsuuT ktiir fi lbeet ?illi byuskun fii
   b. B miš mabsuuT min marra fi lbeet
   c. B raaDi fi lbeet li?annu mabni min lHajar

5. A: biddi beet ma^{c} Hadii?a kbiira wbirkit sbaaHa.
B: bass hadool libyuut γaalyiin ktiir.
A: miš muhim lifluus.
B: kiif biddak tidfa^{c}u, kaaš willa bitta?siiT ?
A: kaaš.
su?aal: bnifham min lHiwaar ?innu ... .
   a. A byištγil mudiir širka
   b. A biHubb ssbaaHa wiTTabii^{c}a
   c. A ^{c}indu ^{c}eela kbiira

Passive participle forms (?ism lmaf^c^uul)

Like English, Arabic has past participle forms that can be used to express passive constructions and adjectives. Consider the following examples:

A. 1. dduxaan mamnuu^c^ hoon meaning (Smoking is forbidden here.)
   2. lmaktab maftuuH meaning (The office is open.)
   3. sayyaarti maSnuu^c^a fi lyaabaan meanng (My car was made in Japan.)

B. 1. beeti mabnii min lHajar meaning (My house is built/made of stone.)
   2. lmayya maɣliyya meaning (The water has been boiled.)

C. 1. ssayyaaraat lmasruu?a btištiɣilš ^c^aadatan meaning (Stolen cars do not usually work.)
   2. l?akil lma?lii biDurr biSSiHHa ktiir meaning (Fried food is very harmful to your health.)

In exampes A, B, and C there are passive participle forms derived from verbs. In A1 the form *mamnu^c^* "forbidden" is derived from *mana^c^*, in A2 *maftuuH* is derived from the verb *fataH,* and in A3 *maSnuu^c^* is derived from the verb *Sana^c^*. In B1 the form *mabni* is derived from the verb *bana,* and in B2 *maɣli* is derived from the verb *ɣala*. In C1 the form *masruu?* is derived from the verb *sara?,* and *ma?lii* is derived from the verb *?ala*. The forms used in groups A and B are passive verb constructions. The examples given in group C function as adjectives describing the the noun phrases that stand for subjects.

There are several patterns of past participles in Arabic. We introduce in this lesson two patterns only; namely, maCCuuC (i.e., *mamnuu^c^, masruu?, maktuub,* etc.) and maCCii (i.e., *maɣlii, ma?lii, mabnii, marmii,* etc.). The pattern maCCuuC is usually derived from the triradical root verbs of the form CVCVC, and the pattern maCCii is derived from the incomplete verbal pattern of the form CaCa. The passive participle, like the active participle, has three forms only: masculine singular, feminine singular, and plural forms. They are also negated by *miš.*

tamriin 5

Fill in the past participle forms of the verbs given in parentheses in the blanks below.

1. ... ssbaaHa hoon. (samaH)
2. lxaTT ... ?ajmal min lxaTT ... . (katab, Taba^c^)
3. widaad bitHubb l?akil ... ktiir. (?ala)
4. ssayyaara ... lalbee^c^. (^c^araD)
5. Saarlu lbeet ... ?aktar min xamis ?ašhur. (sakan)
6. l?akil ... ma^c^ ?ujrit l?uteel. (Hasab)
7. Brenda bti?darš taakul lfawaakih ... . (Tabax)

8. šuft liktaab ... ^{c}ala TTaawla. (rama)

tamriin 6

Provide the verbs from which each of the following past participles forms is derived.

past participle	verb
mašruub	
madruus	
masmuu^{c}	
ma^{c}ruuf	
mahdii	
mad^{c}ii	

tamriin 8

Provide the correct form of the verb in the following sentences:

1. leeš biddik ... sayyaartik ya sihaam ? (baa^{c})
2. ?ana ... ^{c}ala miryam bass ma kaanatiš fi lmaktab. (marr)
3. ?eemta biHibb .... (zaar ?ana)
4. lamma nizil Joe fi ?uteel l-YMCA ... l?akil miš baTTaal. (kaan)
5. ... daayman xadiija taman malaabisha kaašũũ (ydafa^{c})
6. ?ayy sayyaara bidhum ... ? (štara)
7. ?eemta ... ?inta tšuufu ? (?idir)
8. haada lbeet jdiid. miin ... ? (bana lbeet)

tamriin 9

Match the following two columns

^{c}ali buskun fi beet	byaaklu fi lmaktaba
?axuuy biddu	lHajar
TTullaab ^{c}aadatan	l?usbuu^{c} ljaay ?
štarat Hanaan beet maSnuu^{c} min	Hadii?a kbiira ktiir
masaaHit beetna	fii γurufteen bass
?eemta bitkuun faaDi	talaatiin ?alf dinaar bass
^{c}ind l?ustaaz Mike	miiteen mitir mrabba^{c}
si^{c}ir haada lbeet	ybii^{c} beetu

Listen to Tape Segment # 27

HummuS wma?luube

saamya: ween raayHa ya huda ?
huda: raayHa ?a^{c}mal HummuS w?aTbux ma?luube.
saamya: šu! ^{c}indkum Hafla lyoom ?
huda: ya^{c}ni. raayHiin jiraanna yzuuruuna lleela.
saamya: Tayyib. daxlik, kiif bti^{c}mali lHummuS wibtuTubxi lma?luube ?

huda: ^{c}amal lHummuS sihil. ?in?a^{c}i lHummuS fi lmay Hatta ySiir Tari. ba^{c}deen HuTTii fi maakinat xalt wiTHanii. Diifi ^{c}alee šwayyit THiina wišwayyit ^{c}aSiir lamuun. Harki lHummuS w^{c}aSiir llamuun wiTHiina Hatta yinxilTu mniiH. ba^{c}deen Diifi ^{c}alee šwayyit bhaaraat mitil lkammuun ?aw ssimmaak. tinsiiš ?innik tDiifi ^{c}alee šwayyit zeet zeetuun.
saamya: bass! haada ^{c}amalu sihil.
huda: willa, šu bitfakri !
saamya: Tayyib, wkiif btuTubxi lma?luube ?
huda: ?awwal ši ?uslu?i jjaaj ?aw laHmit lxaruuf fi lmay ba^{c}id ma tDiifi ^{c}aleeha raaS baSal mafruum wišwayyit zeet zeetuun. ba^{c}deen ?i?li ?imma baTaaTa ?aw beetinjaan ?aw zahar. lamma txalSi, HuTTi llaHma lmasluu?a fi ?aa^c TTunjara. ba^{c}deen HuTTi Taba?a min rruz foo? llaHma. ba^{c}deen HuTTi Taba?a min lbeetin jaan lma?li. kamli Taba?a foo? Taba?a Hatta twaSli tulteen TTunjara. Diifi mar?at llaHma ^{c}ala rruz willaHma wilbeetinjaan wHuTTi TTunjara ^{c}ala lɣaaz. ?istanni Hawaali nuSS see^{c}a wilma?luube bitkuun jaahza. tinsiiš txalli nnaar xafiifa ^{c}ašaan ma yinHir?iš rruz.
saamya: haadi Tabxa Sa^{c}ba šway.
huda: la?, ?abadan. jarbiiha wšuufi kiif btiTla^c ma^{c}ik.
saamya: wala yhimmik. ?inšaalla raayHa ?aTbuxha l?usbuu^c ljaay. šukran ktiir.
huda: l^{c}afu. bxaaTrik.
saamya: ma^c-i-ssalaama.

lmufradaat

ya^{c}ni	kind of
daxlik	an inceptive marker used to initiate a question or a request
^{c}amal	making
sihil	easy
na?a^{c} (ban?a^{c})	to soak
Tari	soft, tender
TaHan (baTHan)	to grind
Daaf (baDiif)	to add
THiina	sesame butter
xallaT (baxalliT)	to mix
faram (bafrum)	to cut into pieces, to chop
Harrak (baHarrik)	to stir
lamuun	lemon
bhaaraat (sg. bhaar)	spices
kammuun	cumin
simmaak	sumac
nisi (bansa)	to forget
zeet zeetuun	olive oil
willa	of course
γaaz	burner
sala? (baslu?)	to boil
raas baSal	an onion head
?alaa (ba?li)	to fry
?imma	either
zahar	cauliflower
beetinjaan	eggplants
?aa^{c}	bottom
Tunjara	cooking pot
Taba?a	a layer
foo?	on top of
ma?li	fried (adj.)
masluu?	boiled (adj.)
mara?a	broth
Hara? (baHri?)	to burn
xafiif	light

naar	fire
?inHara? (baniHri?)	to get burnt
?abadan	not at all
jarrab (bajarrib)	to try
Tili^{c} (baTla^{c})	to become

Other vocabulary found in the following exercises or on tape

tkawwan	to be made of
min ?eeš	of what ... ?
muHtawayaat	contents, ingredients
laHmit ^{c}ijil	beef
ba^{c}D	some
suuši	a Japanese dish
mašhuur	popular, famous
?akla	dish
dili^{c}	plain
milH	salt
Ta^{c}im	taste
γariib	strange
min ?abil	before
Siiγa (pl. Siyaγ)	form
fi^{c}il (?af^{c}aal)	verb
been ?useen	between brackets
ba?doonis	parsley
?uuma	Indian female name
Haarr	spicy, hot
waa?il	Arabic male name
Tabiix	cooked food
SaraTa	salad
ša?fa (pl. šu?af)	a piece
fawzi	Arabic male name
?ahwe saada	black coffee with no sugar
sukkar	sugar
mHammar	roasted
?illi biddak ?iyyaa	whatever you want
min ?abil	before
?aTa^{c} (ba?Ta^{c})	to cut

HaTT (baHuTT)	to put
furn (pl. fruun)	a stove
rγiif (pl. turuufa)	a loaf of bread
r?ii?	thin
madhuun	rubbed with
rajja^c (barajji^c)	to send, put, take back

tamriin 1

jaawib ^{c}ala l?as?ila ttaalya.

1. šu raayHa ti^{c}mal huda ?
2. leeš raayHa ti^{c}mal huda HummuS wtuTbux ma?luube ?
3. kiif bin^{c}amal lHummuS ?
4. bti^{c}raf saamya ti^{c}mal HummuS ?
5. kiif btinTabax lma?luube ?
6. miin ?ashal ^{c}amal lHummuS willa Tabx lma?luube ?
7. šu muHtawayaat SaHin lHummuS ?
8. min ?eeš btitkawwan Tabxit lma?luube ?

tamriin 2

?ixtaar ljawaab SSaHiiH.

1. bidha huda ti^{c}mal HummuS wtuTbux ma?luube li?annu ... .
   a. ^{c}indha Hafla b. saamya raayHa tzuurha
   c. jiraanha raayHiin yzuruuha
2. lamma bni^{c}mal HummuS, ?awwal ši ... .
   a. binxalliT lHummuS b. bnin?a^c lHummuS
   c. binDiif THiina ^{c}ala lHummuS
3. lma?luube Tabxa ... .
   a. filisTiiniyya b. maSriyya
   c. maγribiyya
4. bnin?a^c ^{c}aadatan lHummuS fi ... .
   a. zeet zzeetuun b. ^{c}aSiir lamuun
   c. mayy
5. fi Tabxit lma?luube byista^{c}imlu nnaas ^{c}aadatan ... .
   a. laHmit xaruuf ?aw jaaj b. laHmit xaruuf ?aw ^{c}ijil
   c. laHmit ^{c}ijil ?aw jaaj
6. btaaxud Tabxit lma?luube ^{c}aadatan ... ta?riiban.
   a. nuSS see^{c}a b. see^{c}a wnuSS c. talat see^{c}aat

7. ^{c}ašaan nuTbux ma?luube laazim ... ?awwal ši.

   a. ni?li llaHma b. nuslu? beetinjaan

   c. nuslu? llaHma

8. bnuTbux lma?luube ^{c}aadatan fi ... .

   a. lmayy b. mar?at llaHma

   c. zeet zeetuun

tamriin 3

?ixtaar ljawaab SSaHiiH.

1. nnaas ... llaHma fi lmayy.

   a. byi?lu b. byuslu?u

2. nnaas ^{c}aadatan ... lHummuS.

   a. bixalTu b. byufurmu

3. l?ameerkaan ... ketchup ^{c}ala lhaamburger.

   a. biHarku b. biDiifu

4. ma ?ajaaš ?aHmad ^{c}ala lHafla li?annu ... .

   a. nisi b. Tili^{c}

5. lamma bnuTbux wara? ^{c}inab bnista^{c}mil ... .

   a. maaknit xalT b. Tunjara

6. ba^{c}D nnaas ... kammuun ^{c}ala lHummuS.

   a. bufurmu b. biDiifu

7. ^{c}abdalla biHubb ... ktiir.

   a. lmara?a b. lma?li

8. ?alat mbaariH warda samkateen fi ... .

   a. zeet zeetuun b. lmayy

9. kariim biHubb yaakul ... .

   a. mara?a b. beetinjaan

10. šuft jamiila ... raas baSal.

   a. bti^{c}mal b. btufrum

tamriin 4

?i?ra lHiwaaraat ttaaliya wjaawib ^{c}ala l?as?ila taHthum.

1. A: ween kunt ya ^{c}abid ?

   ^{c}abid: kunt ?atγadda.

   A: ?addeeš kallafak lγada ?

   ^{c}abid: xamis ta^{c}šar dulaar.

   su?aal: tγadda ^{c}abid fi beetu willa fi maT^{c}am ? kiif ^{c}rift ?

2. A: šu ?akalti ᶜala lifTuur ya Sally ?
Sally: ma ?akaltiš lifTuur.
su?aal: ?addeeš kallaf fTuur Sally ?

3. A: šu btaakul ya Brad ?
Brad: suuši.
A: min ween štareetu ?
Brad: ?ana Tabaxtu.
A: kiif tᶜallamt tuTubxu ?
Brad: sakant fi lyaabaan ?aktar min sana.
su?aal: ween tᶜallam Brad yuTbux suuši ?

4. A: šu haada ?
B: baaba γannuuj.
A: šu yaᶜni baaba γannuuj ?
B: ?akla mašhuura fi suuriyya wlubnaan.
su?aal: miin byaakul ᶜaadatan baaba γannuuj ?

5. A: haada l?akil diliᶜ, fii ᶜindkum miliH ?
B: tfaDDal, haada lmilH.
su?aal: kiif biHubb A ?aklu ?

6. A: šu fii fi l?akil, Taᶜmu γariib ?
B: summaak.
A: šu yaᶜni summaak ?
B: nooᶜ min libhaar mašhuur fi ššarq l?awsaT.
su?aal: kam marra ?akal B summaak min ?abil ?

lmabni lilmajhuul (Passive Constructions)

The verb *nHara?* in the sentence *"tinsiiš txalli nnaar xafiifa ᶜašaan ma yinHir?iš rruz"* is in the passive form. The corresponding active form is *Hara?* "to burn." Passive forms are as common in this dialect of Arabic as they are in English or in any other language for that matter. There are two prefixes that can be used to transform an active verb into a passive one. The first prefix is *?in-* where *?i-* is usually dropped (not pronounced). This prefix is usually added to the triradical active transitive verbs such as *katab, širib, ᶜimil, zakar, fataH, masak, Hamal, dafaᶜ, fihim,* and *?ibil,* and the incomplete verbs such as *bana, štara,* and *γaza,* which become *?inbana, ?inšara,*

?inɣaza, respectively. The other prefix is *t-* which is usually added to transitive verbs whose middle radical is geminated and the verb of the form CaaCaC such as *šaarak, ᶜaašar,* and *naafas.* For example, the active verbs *ra??a, waZZaf, sakkar, wassaᶜ, xarrab,* and *SallaH* become *tra??a, twaZZaf, tsakkar, twassaᶜ, txarrab, tSallaH,* respectively. Triradical verbs starting with /?/ take the prefix /*t-*/ instead of the expected /*?in-*/. Examples of this type are *?axad* and *?akal* whose passive forms are *ttaaxad* and *ttaakal,* respectively. Passive verbs are conjugated in a way similar to the active ones. The following illustrate the conjugation.

The verb *tra??a* with the prefix *t-*

pronoun	past/perfect	imperfect	subjunctive
?ana	tra??eet	batra??a	?atra??a
?inta	tra??eet	btitra??a	titra??a
?inti	tra??eeti	btitra??i	titra??i
huwwe	tra??a	bitra??a	yitra??a
hiyye	tra??at	btitra??a	titra??a
?iHna	tra??eena	bnitra??a	nitra??a
?intu	tra??eetu	btitra??u	titra??u
humme	tra??u	byitra??u	yitra??u

The verb *nmasak* with the prefix *?in-*

?ana	nmasakt	banimsik	?animsik
?inta	nmasakt	btinimsik	tinimsik
?inti	nmasakti	btinmiski	tinmiski
huwwe	nmasak	binimsik	yinimsik
hiyye	nmaskat	btinimsik	tinimsik
?iHna	nmasakna	bninimsik	ninimsik
?intu	nmasaktu	btinmisku	tinmisku
humme	nmasaku	binmisku	yinmisku

Passive verbs are negated in a manner identical to that of the active ones. Thus, the perfect forms are negated by adding *ma* before the verb and *-š* at the end of the verb, and *-š* is added to the end of the imperfect indicative verb.

tamriin 5

?ixtaar ljawaab SSaHiiH.

1. rrisaala ... ?abil yoomeen.
   a. katbat b. nkatbat
2. ... Ibraahiim lbaab.
   a. fataH b. nfataH
3. lfaatuura ... ?abil ma wSilt.
   a. daf^{c}at b. ndaf^{c}at
4. ... ?aHmad fi bank lqaahira-^{c}ammaan fi l?urdun.
   a. waZZaf b. twaZZaf
5. miin ... lHummuS ?
   a. ^{c}imil b. n^{c}amal
6. ?eemta ... lHummuS ?
   a. ^{c}imil b. n^{c}amal
7. ma Dalliš ?ahwe min marra. ... kulha.
   a. širbit b. nšarbat
8. ... lma?luube fi beet samiir kull ?usbuu^{c} ta?riiban
   a. btuTbux b. btinTabax
9. haada lbeet ... bi $100,000.
   a. štara b. nšara
10. ^{c}adnaan ... ^{c}aSiir ttufaaH ^{c}ala lifTuur.
    a. širib b. nšarab

tamriin 6

?a^{c}Ti SSiiγa SSaHiiHa lakull fi^{c}il min l?af^{c}aal lmawjuuda been ?useen.

1. ^{c}ašaan ni^{c}mal HummuS laazim ... lHummuS fi lmayy Tuul lleel. (na?a^{c})
2. stanna laHZa! ba^{c}d šwayy raayiH (?ana) ... lmiliH ^{c}ala l?akil. (Daaf)
3. lamma bni^{c}mal HummuS, ... lHummuS wiTHiina w^{c}aSiir llamuun. (xallaT)
4. ... James kull yoom SSubH beeDteen. (?alaa)
5. ?abil ma štara ^{c}aadil wzoojtu sayyaarithum ?ista?jaru ?aktar min xamis sayyaaraat w... . (jarrab)
6. lamma HaDDarat Hilwa tabbuula yoom ssabat lmaaDi, ?awwal ši ... lba?doonis. (faram)
7. kiif btuTbuxi jjaaj ya samiira, ... willa bti?lii ? (sala?)
8. ?eemta raayHa ... lmajisteer ya ^{c}abiir ? (kammal)

The Imperative Form

Consider the following verbs:

perfect form	imperative form
katab	?uktub
sabaH	?isbaH
maša	?imši
^{c}aamal	^{c}aamil
kaasar	kaasir
sakkar	sakkir
raaH	ruuH
^{c}aaš	^{c}iiš
daar	duur
?ista^{c}mal	?ista^{c}mil
?ista?jar	?ista?jir
ma katabš	(ma) tuktubš
ma raHš	(ma) truHš
ma mašaaš	(ma) timšiiš
ma γallabš	(ma) tγallibš
ma širbiš	(ma) tišrabš

Based on these data, form the rules that determine the formation of the imperatives in this dialect of Arabic. An example of a rule could be: Add the prefix *?i-* to the beginning of the triradical consonant root to form the imperative, e.g., fataH ---> ?iftaH.

The instructor will discuss these rules with you in class after you have come up with them by yourself at home.

tamriin 7

While taking care of a ten-year-old boy, you decide to provide him with a set of rules as to what he can and cannot do. These rules are given in the form of commands. Write down twelve of these. The following two examples illustrate what the rules should be like.

-tiftaHiš lbaab min marra!
-?udrus haada liktaab halla!

tamriin 8

1. Describe the way you go about preparing your favorite meal.
2. A friend from overseas asks you for a recipe for cheesecake. Write down that recipe for her. Use the dictionary to look up any new vocabulary that you may need.

Listen to Tape Segment # 28

madiinat-i-l?uds

taqa^{c} madiinat l?uds fi minTa?a jabaliyya ^{c}ala bu^{c}ud xamsiin keelumitir ta?riiban min sawaaHil lbaHar l?abyaD lmutawassiT ššar?iyya. tamtaaz lmadiina bitaariixha l^{c}ariiq w?ahammiyyitha ttaariixiyya waddiiniyya. hiyye min ?a?dam w?a?das mudun l^{c}aalam. banaaha lyabuusiyyiin min ?aktar min 3000 sana ?abil lmiilaad. wmin hadaak lwa?t whiyye markaz Siraa^{c} lakull l?umam wišsu^{c}uub widdiyaanaaat. ?iddammarat lmadiina ^{c}iddit marraat wsukkaanha Saaru ?asra fi ^{c}iddit munaasabaat. wma^{c} zaalik, laa zaalat lmadiina Hayya wibyuskunha ?aktar min nuSS malyoon nasama halla.

madiinat l?uds

l?uds ma?suuma ?ismeen: l?uds l?adiima wil?uds jdiida. fii Hawl l?uds l?adiima Suur Daxm banaa l?atraak ?abil Hawaali ?arba^{c} miit sana. masaaHit lmadiina Hawaali keelumitir mrabba^{c} waaHad. ššwaari^{c} hunaak Day?a w^{c}aadatan mas?uufa. fii dakaakiin zγiira ktiir fi lmadiina: dakaakiin tuHaf, wmujawharaat, wba??aalaat, wmaTaa^{c}im, wmaHallaat Halwayaat, wmaHallaat nuvuteeh, wmaHallaat ?maaš, wmaHallaat see^{c}aat.

qubbat SSaxra

kniisit li?yaama

Haa?iT lmabka

fi lmadiina ?aHyaa? ktiira. ?ašhar haadi l?aHyaa? ?arba^{c}a: lHayy l?islaami, lHayy lmasiiHi, lHayy lyahuudi, wilHayy l?armani. fiiha kamaan maraakiz m?addasa qliddiyaanaat ssamaawiyya ttalaata: lmasjid l?aqSa wqubbat SSaxra lilmisilmiin, kniisit li?yaama lilmasiiHiyyiin, wHaa?iT lmabka lilyahuud. ᶜašaan heek fii fi l?uds ᶜaadatan suwwaaH ?aktar min sukkaanha wfiiha kamaan ?utelaat ktiira. winnaas hunaak byitkallamu ᶜaadatan talat luɣaat: lᶜarabiyya wil?ingliiziyya, wilᶜibriyya. lHa?ii?a ?innu ?iqtiSaad lmadiina manbi ᶜala ssiyaaHa wittijaara bass.

fii la l?uds l?adiima sabaᶜ madaaxil, hiyya baab lᶜamuud, wbaab zzaahra, wbaab lisbaaT, wbaab lmaɣaarba, wbaab nnabi dahuud, wbaab lxaliil, wilbaab lijdiid.

baab lᶜamuud

lbaab lijdiid

l?uds jdiida mitil ?ayy madiina jdiida. šawaariᶜha ᶜariiDa wbinaayaatha ᶜaalya wmasaaHitha ?akbar biktiir min l?uds l?adiima, wfiiha kamaan muntazahaat mniiHa wmaHallaat tijaariyya kbiira.

TTa?s fi l?uds Hilu Tuul ssana. fi SSeef ljaww mumtaaz ktiir. daayman mušmis wjaaff wfii hunaak ᶜaadatan nasiim byiiji min lɣarb, min lbaHar lmutawassiT. fi ššita bikuun ?aHyaanan baarid šway w?aHyaanan mušmis wdaafi. marraat btinzil darjat lHaraara ᶜan SSifr lmi?awi w?aHyaanan bikuun TTa?s ᶜaaSif, bass haada ?aliil.

baab SbaaT

Tarii? l?aalaam

lmufradaat

taqa^c	to lie, to be situated
^cala bu^cd	at a distance
saaHil (pl. sawaaHil)	shore
tamtaaz	to be distinguished
^cariiq	ancient
?ahammiyya	importance
yabuusiyyiin	Jebusites (the people who founded Jerusalem)
?abil lmiilaad	before Christ (i.e., B. C.)
markaz (pl. maraakiz)	center
Siraa^c	conflict
ša^cb (pl. šu^cuub)	people
?umma (pl. ?umam)	a nation
?iddammar	to be destroyed
?asiir (pl. ?asraa)	captive
munaasaba (pl. munaasabaat)	occasion
ma^c zaalik	though, despite that
laa zaal	still
Hayy	alive
malyoon	a million
nasama	a person
m?addas	holy
^caalam	the world
qisim	part, portion
ma?suum	divided
Hawl	around
Suur	a wall
Daxm	huge
banaa	to build, to construct
turki (pl. ?atraak)	Turks
masaaHa	area
mas?uuf	roofed
mjawharaat	jewelry
?i?maaš	cloth
lHa?ii?a	the truth, in fact
?iqtiSaad	economy
mabni	is built

siyaaHa	tourism
tijaara	trade
Hayy (pl. ?aHyaa?)	a quarter
masiiHi	a Christian
yahuudi	a Jew, Jewish
markaz (pl. maraakiz)	center
diin (pl. diyaanaat, ?adyaan)	religion
?armani	Armenian
lmasjid l?aqSa	the Aqsa Mosque
qubbat SSaxra	Dome of the Rock
kniisit li?yaama	the Church of Holy Sepulchre
Haa?iT lmabka	the Wailing Wall
sukkaan	dwellers, population
nabi	prophet
dahuud	David
mitil	like, such as
muntazah (pl. muntazahaat)	a park

Other vocabulary found in the following exercises or on tape

beeš	for what
^{c}abr	through (the ages)
^{c}adad	number
?i^{c}tamad	to be based
Sinaa^{c}a	industry
mu^{c}Zam	most
?aθar (?aaθaar)	ruins
kibir (bakbar)	to grow
Harb lxaliij	the Gulf War
maSna^{c} (pl. maSaani^{c})	a factory
^{c}ala ?eeš	on what ... ?
jamaal	beauty
burj	tower
šaaTi? (pl. šawaaTi?)	beach
ramil	sand
ramli	sandy
burtuγaali	Portuguese
?aθiina	Athens

tamriin 1

jaawib ^{c}ala l?as?ila ttaaliya min lqiT^{c}a.

1. ween btaqa^{c} madiinat l?uds ?
2. beeš btimtaaz lmadiina ?
3. miin bana l?uds ?
4. šu Saar la l?uds ^{c}abr l^{c}uSuur ?
5. ?addeeš ^{c}adad sukkaan lmadiina halla ?
6. waSSif lmadiina l?adiima.
7. kam Hayy fii fi lmadiina l?adiima ? šu humme ?
8. šu ?ahammiyyit lmadiina min nnaaHiya ddiiniyya ?
9. leeš fii fi l?uds ?utelaat ktiira ?
10. kam madxal fi la lmadiina l?adiima ? šu humme ?
11. kiif btixtlif lmadiina jdiida ^{c}an l?adiima ?
12. kiif ljaww fi l?uds ?

tamriin 2

?ixtaar ljawaab SSaHiiH.

1. tarji^{c} ?ahammiyyat l?uds likawnha .... .
   a. markaz liddiyaanaat ssamaawiyya ttalaata
   b. taqa^{c} fi minTa?a jabaliyya
2. l?uds ma?suuma ?ismiin, humme .... .
   a. ?ism lmisilmiin w?ism lmasiiHiyyiin
   b. lmadiina l?adiima wilmadiina jdiida
3. fii la l?uds l?adiima .... .
   a. saba^{c} madaaxil
   b. saba^{c} ?aHyaa?
4. ?ašhar lmaraakiz lma?adasa ^{c}ind lmisilmiin huwwe ..
   a. Haa?iT lmabka
   b. qubbat SSaxra
5. byi^{c}tamid ?iqtiSaad l?uds ^{c}ala .... .
   a. ttijaara wiSSinaa^{c}a
   b. ssiyaaHa wittijaara
6. l?uds fiiha ?utelaat ktiira li?annu .... .
   a. byiiji ^{c}aleeha suyyaaH ktiir kull sana
   b. fii Hawlha Suur Daxim banaa l?atraak
7. TTa?s fi l?uds fi SSeef .... .
   a. Hilu ktiir

b. mušmis bass raTib

8. min ?ašhar kanaayis l?uds ... .

   a. qubbit SSaxra

   b. kniisit li?yaama

9. ᶜumur l?uds ... ta?riiban.

   a. 3000 sana

   b. 5000 sana

10. ššawaariᶜ fi l?uds jdiida ... .

   a. Day?a wmas?uufa

   b. ᶜariiDa wikbiira

tamriin 3

?ixtaar ljawaab SSaHiiH (Review the vocabulary words and their uses before you start to answer this exercise.)

1. lqaahira ... ᶜala nahr nniil.

   a. taqaᶜ   b. btinzil

2. tamtaaz maSir bitaariixha ... .

   b. DDaxm   b. lᶜariiq

3. ?addeeš ᶜadad ... madiinat New York ?

   a. sukkaan   b. zabaayin

4. ?ištara yuusuf ?amiiSu min maHal ... .

   a. tuHaf   b. ?i?maaš

5. lmasjid l?aqSa min lmaraakiz ddiiniyya lmuhimma ᶜind ... .

   a. lmisilmiin   b. lmasiiHiyyiin

6. ?iHna bništri ?akilna min ... .

   a. ba??aala   b. maHal mujawharaat

7. byiᶜtamid ?iqtiSaad lmadiina ᶜala ... ?iza bikuun fiiha ?utelaat ktiira.

   a. SSinaaᶜa   b. ssiyaaHa

8. SSiin ?akbar balad fi ... .

   a. lᶜaalam   b. ?ooroobba

9. muᶜZam nnaas fi Canada ... .

   a. yahuud   b. masiHiyyiin

10. fii fi Chicago ᶜašar ... .

   a. ?aHyaa?   b. binaayaat

A Different Variety of Spoken Arabic

The passage *madiinat l?uds* combines elements from Levantine Arabic and elements from Modern Standard Arabic (MSA). These elements include sounds, words, phrases, and grammatical markers such as negation markers. This passage is a sample of a variety of Arabic called Educated Spoken Arabic (ESA). ESA is neither a pure vernacular variety nor pure MSA. It is an interplay in which the speaker switches back and forth between the two varieties in a way intuitive to him and to the listener. Consider the following examples from the passage cited for illustration.

Elements from the passage	Their equivalents in vernacular Arabic
taqa^c madiinat l?usd	bti?a^c madiinat l?uds ....
tamtaaz lmadiina bitaariixha l^{c}ariiq	btitmayyaz lmadiina btaariixha l?adiim ktiir
... laa zaalat lmadiina Hayya	kamaaha lamdiina Hayya
... ?iqitiSaad lmadiina mabni ^{c}ala ...	byi^{c}tmid ?iqtiSaad lamdiina ^{c}ala ...

Note also how the following words retain the sound /q/:

1. ?iqtiSaad not ?i?tiSaad
2. l?aqSa not l?a?Sa

There are two varieties of ESA: regional ESA and inter-regional or inter-dialectal ESA. Regional ESA, which is represented by the passage *madiinat l?uds,* is the elevated style used by the educated Arab speakers of any region when they are involved in an intellectual discussion or a semi-formal talk, description, or narration. This variety is usually determined by the topic, the setting, and the level of education of the interlocutors. Inter-dialectal ESA stands for a form of oral communication used by the educated Arab speakers of various regional dialects. This variety is characterized by combining elements from the various local vernacular varieties and MSA. Other processes used in this variety are leveling of differences through negotiation for meaning, elimination of lexical items that are restricted in their use to one region only, avoidance of stigmatized vernacular forms, and so on. The exact rules that determine which elements will be included or excluded have not been regularized yet.

The passage *madiinat l?uds* represents, as mentioned above, a sample of the regional ESA. Like inter-regional ESA, the rules of switching back and forth have not been formed yet. Therefore, it might be advisable at this stage that we study each passage by itself focusing on how different it is from Levantine Arabic without attempting to regularize the differences.

tamriin 4

Determine whether the following utterances belong to colloquial Levantine Arabic or not and provide the reason for your answer. (Hint: If some of the words in the sentence are not familiar to you, the construction is most likely to be non-Levantine Arabic.)

1. ?aSbaHat madiinat lquds markaz Siraa^{c} lakull ššu^{c}uub.
2. dummirat lquds ^{c}iddit marraat.
3. ^{c}ašaan heek fii fi l?uds suwwaaH ?aktar min sukkaanha.
4. maqsuuma lmadiina qismayn.
5. fii fi l?uds ?aHyaa? ktiira.
6. l?uds b^{c}iida ^{c}an lbaHr lmutawassiT xamsiin keelumitir bass.
7. yuujad fi lquds ?amaakin muqaddasa likull ddiyaanaat.
8. btinzilš darjat lHaraara ^{c}an SSifir min marra fi riiHa

tamriin 5

Study the following sentences carefully and classify the verbs in each of these sentences into Levantine or Standard Arabic based on their features.

1. ?ana ?atakallmu lfaransiyya wal^{c}arabiyya wal?isbaaniyya.
2. Ann taskunu fi šaari^{c} Williams.
3. ?aHmad byaakul kull yoom fi maT^{c}am Wendy's.
4. humme bidaxnuuš min marra.
5. nnaas byil^{c}abu ttinis ktiir fi ?ooroobba.
6. lam tasbaH saara l?usbuu^{c} lmaaDi.
7. ?ayy kitaab darasta yoom ssabt ?
8. ?atuHibbu ?an ta?kula HummuS ?
9. ?ayyu jariidatan taqra?iin ya naadya ?
10. hiyye miš raayHa tsaafir ba^{c}id šahreen.

tamriin 6

Go through the passage and list all the words, phrases, and sentences that are non-Levantine or Standard Arabic. For example, in analyzing the first sentence we can say that the whole sentence with the exception of the word *minTa?a* belongs to Standard Arabic.

tamriin 7

The picture below shows the city of Vancouver. Describe the city as it is shown in the picture.

tamriin 8

The following are brief descriptions of major world cities. Your task is to identify these cities based on the descriptions given here.

1. taqa^{c} ^{c}ala saaHil lwilaayaat lmutaHidda ššarqi. fiiha binaayaat ^{c}aalya ktiira. fiiha kamaan mabna l?ummam lmutaHida wtimsaal lHuriyya.
   šu hiyye haadi lamdiina ?
2. madiina kbiira ktiir fi januub ɣarb lwilaayaat lmutaHida, bijuuz tkuun ?akbar madiina fi ?ameerka. ?ariiba ^{c}ala madiinat Holywood.
   šu hiyye haadi lmadiina ?
3. madiina mašhuura bitaariixha l^{c}ariiq wib?aaswaarha l?adiima. nnaas hunaak byitkallamu ?iTaali. fiiha kamaan ?aham markaz liddiin lamsiiHi, lvatikaan.
   šu hiyye haadi lamdiina ?
4. taqa^{c} fi ?ooroobba. kaanat ma?asuuma ?ismeen, l?ism ššar?i wil?ism lɣarbi. kaan hunaak Suur Daxm been l?ism ššar?i wil?ism lɣarbi. ?iddamar SSuur sant 1989 wSaarat madiina waHada. nnaas byitkallamu hunaak ?almaani.
   šu hiyye haadi lmadiina ?
5. nnaas hunaak byitkallmau ^{c}arabi. mašhuura lmadiina bitaariixha l?adiim. fiiha ?aasaar ktiira xuSuuSan l?ahraam. taqa^{c} ^{c}ala nahr nniil.
   šu hiyye haadi lmadiina ?

tamriin 9

Write a one-page description of your hometown similar to the one given in the passage above.

Listen to Tape Segment #29

Appendix A

Verb Conjugation in Levantine Arabic

The following is a list of the verb patterns covered in this course and their conjugation. Each pattern is designated by a consonant-vowel (CV) form followed by vowel alternations, when alternations are applicable, and a member verb. The CV form and the member verb designating the pattern are given in the third person singular perfect form (the standard form generally used by Arab grammarians and Arabists), and the vowel alternation represents the perfect-imperfect changes that accompany the conjugation. Note that the list provided below is limited to the patterns introduced in this course only. For a detailed list consult a reference book of grammar for this dialect.

A. Triradical Verbs

1. The Model **CaCaC (a~u), e.g., daras/byudrus**

Pronoun	Past Tense	Present Tense	Subjunctive	Imperative
?ana	darast	badrus	?adrus	....
?inta	darast	btudrus	tudrus	?udrus
?inti	darasti	btudursi	tudursi	?udursi
huwwe	daras	b(y)udrus	yudrus	....
hiyye	darsat	btudrus	tudrus	....
?iHna	darasna	bnudrus	nudrus	....
?intu	darastu	btudursu	tudursu	?udursu
humme	darasu	b(y)udursu	yudursu	....

Verbs that can be conjugated similarly are:

katab	daxal	xaraj	?a^c^ad
zakar	?amar	šakar	HaDar

2. The Model **CaCaC (a~a), e.g., sabaH/byisbaH**

Pronoun	Past Tense	Present Tense	Subjunctive	Imperative
?ana	sabaHt	basbaH	?asbaH	....
?inta	sabaHt	btisbaH	tisbaH	?isbaH
?inti	sabaHti	btisbaHi	tisbaHi	?isbaHi
huwwe	sabaH	b(y)isbaH	yisbaH	....
hiyye	sabHat	btisbaH	tisbaH	....
?iHna	sabaHna	bnisbaH	nisbaH	....
?intu	sabaHtu	btisbaHu	tisbaHu	?isbaHu
humme	sabaHu	b(y)isbaHu	yisbaHu	....

Verbs that can be conjugated similarly are dafa^c^, fataH, and naSaH

3. The Model **CaCaC (a~i) e.g., Hasab/byiHsib**

Pronoun	Past Tense	Present Tense	Subjunctive	Imperative
?ana	Hasabt	baHsib	?aHsib	....
?inta	Hasabt	btiHsib	tiHsib	?iHsib
?inti	Hasabti	btiHisbi	tiHisbi	?iHisbi
huwwe	Hasab	byiHsib	yiHsib	....
hiyye	Hasbat	btiHsib	tiHsib	....
?iHna	Hasabna	bniHsib	niHsib	....
?intu	Hasabtu	btiHisbu	tiHisbu	?iHisbu
humme	Hasabu	byiHisbu	yiHisbu	....

Verbs that can be conjugated similarly are:

masak Hamal ^{c}azam hajam Hara?

4. The model **CiCiC (i~a), e.g., širib/byišrab**

Pronoun	Past Tense	Present Tense	Subjunctive	Imperative
?ana	šribt	bašrab	?ašrab	....
?inta	šribt	btišrab	tišrab	?išrab
?inti	šribti	btišrabi	tišrabi	?išrabi
huwwe	širib	b(y)išrab	yišrab	....
hiyye	širbit	btišrab	tišrab	....
?iHna	šribna	bnišrab	nišrab	....
?intu	šribtu	btišrabu	tišrabu	?išrabu
humme	širbu	b(y)išrabu	yišrabu	....

Verbs that can be conjugated similarly are:

Tili^{c} riji^{c} li^{c}ib zi^{c}il ?ibil

simi^{c} ^{c}imil ?idir rikib sihir

fihim

5. The model **CiCiC (i~i), e.g., libis/byilbis**

Pronoun	Past Tense	Present Tense	Subjunctive	Imperative
?ana	lbist	balbis	?albis	....
?inta	lbist	btilbis	tilbis	?ilbis
?inti	lbisti	btilbisi	tilbisi	?ilbisi
huwwe	libis	byilbis	yilbis	....
hiyye	libsit	btilbis	tilbis	....
?iHna	lbisna	bnilbis	nilbis	....
?intu	lbistu	btilbisu	tilbisu	?ilbisu
humme	libsu	byilbisu	yilbisu	....

Verbs that can be conjugated similarly are nizil, ^{c}irif, and wiSil.

B. Augmented Triradical Verbs

1. The Model **CaCCaC (a-a~a-i), e.g., sakkar/bisakkir**

Pronoun	Past Tense	Present Tense	Subjunctive	Imperative
?ana	sakkart	basakkir	?asakkir	....
?inta	sakkart	bitsakkir	tsakkir	sakkir
?inti	sakkarti	bitsakri	tsakri	sakri
huwwe	sakkar	bisakkir	ysakkir	....
hiyye	sakkarat	bitsakkir	tsakkir	....
?iHna	sakkarna	binsakkir	nsakkir	....
?intu	sakkartu	bitsakru	tsakru	sakru
humme	sakkaru	bisakru	tsakru	....

Verbs that can be conjugaged similarly are:

kattab	^{c}allam	darras	xarrab	kazzab
waHHad	?ajjar	^{c}azzab	zakkar	?a^{cc}ad
daxxal	daxxan	rajja^{c}	saffar	sabbaH

2. The Model **CaaCaC (aa-a ~ aa-i), e.g., saafar/bisaafir**

Pronoun	Past Tense	Present Tense	Subjunctive	Imperative
?ana	saafart	basaafir	?asaafir	....
?inta	saafart	bitsaafir	tsaafir	saafir
?inti	saafarti	bitsaafri	tsaafri	saafri
huwwe	saafar	bisaafir	ysaafir	....
hiyye	saafarat	bitsaafir	tsaafir	....
?iHna	saafarna	binsaafir	nsaafir	....
?intu	saafartu	bitsaafru	tsaafru	saafru
humme	saafaru	bisaafru	ysaafru	....

Verbs that can be conjugated similarly are:

kaatab	šaarak	^{c}aamal	^{c}aašar
daafa^{c}	?aatal	kaasar	naafas

3. The model **tCaCCaC, e.g., tkallam/byitkallam**

Pronoun	Past Tense	Present Tense	Subjunctive	Imperative
?ana	tkallamt	batkallam	?aatkallam	....
?inta	tkallamt	btitkallam	titkallam	tkallam
?inti	tkallamti	btitkallami	titkallami	tkallami
huwwe	tkallam	byitkallam	yitkallam	....
hiyye	tkallamat	btitkallam	titkallam	....
?iHna	tkallamna	bnitkallam	nitkallam	....
?intu	tkallamtu	btitkallamu	titkallamu	tkallamu
humme	tkallamu	byitkallamu	yitkallamu	....

Verbs that can be conjugated similarly are:

trayyaH	tjawwal	tšammas	tHammam
t^{c}arraf	tšarraf	tfarraj ^{c}ala	t^{c}allam

4. The model **(?i)staCCaC (a-a~a-i), e.g., (?i)sta?jar/byista?jir**

Pronoun	Past Tense	Present Tense	Subjunctive	Imperative
?ana	sta?jar	basta?jir	?asta?jir	....
?inta	sta?jar	byista?jir	yista?jir	sta?jir
?inti	sta?jarti	btista?ijri	tista?ijri	sta?ijri
huwwe	sta?jar	basta?jir	yista?jir	....
hiyye	sta?jarat	btista?jir	tista?jir	....
?iHna	sta?jarna	bnista?jir	nista?jir	....
?intu	sta?jartu	btista?ijru	tista?ijru	sta?ijru
humme	sta?jaru	byista?ijru	yista?ijru	....

Verbs that can be conjugated similarly are:

sta^{c}mal stahlak stab^{c}ad staγrab

C. Hollow Verbs

1. The Model **CaaC (aa~uu), e.g., raaH/biruuH**

Pronoun	Past Tense	Present Tense	Subjunctive	Imperative
?ana	ruHt	baruuH	?aruuH	....
?inta	ruHt	bitruuH	truuH	ruuH
?inti	ruHti	bitruuHi	truuHi	ruuHi
huwwe	raaH	biruuH	yruuH	....
hiyye	raaHt	bitruuH	truuH	....
?iHna	ruHna	binruuH	nruuH	....
?intu	ruHtu	bitruuHu	truuHu	ruuHu
humme	raaHu	biruuHu	yruuHu	....

Verbs that can be conjugated similarly are:

?aal ?aam šaaf zaar saa? daar

2. The Model **CaaC, e.g., naam/binaam.** Note though that five of the perfect forms have /i/ rather than /aa/. Therefore, the pattern shows some alternation.

Pronoun	Past Tense	Present Tense	Subjunctive	Imperative
?ana	nimt	banaam	?anaam	....
?inta	nimt	bitnaam	tnaam	naam
?inti	nimti	bitnaami	tnaami	naami
huwwe	naam	binaam	ynaam	....
hiyye	naamat	bitnaam	tnaam	....
?iHna	nimna	binnaam	nnaam	....

?intu	nimtu	bitnaamu	tnaamu	naamu
humme	naamu	binaamu	ynaamu	....

3. The Model **CaaC (aa~ii), e.g., Taab/biTiib.** Note that /i/, not /aa/, is used in five perfect forms. The vowel alternations is limited to only some forms.

Pronoun	Past Tense	Present Tense	Subjunctive	Imperative
?ana	Tibt	baTiib	?aTiib	....
?inta	Tibt	biTiib	tTiib	Tiib
?inti	Tibt	bitTiibi	tTiibi	Tiibi
huwwe	Taab	biTiib	yTiib	....
hiyye	Taabat	biTiib	tTiib	....
?iHna	Tibna	binTiib	tTiib	Tiibu
?intu	Tibtu	biTiibu	tTiibu	....
humme	Taabu	biTiibu	tTiibu	....

Verbs that can be conjugated similarly are:
saab ᶜaaš baaᶜ Taab Daaᶜ

D. Incomplete Verbs

1. The Model **CaCa (a~i), e.g., Haka/byiHki**

Pronoun	Past Tense	Present Tense	Subjunctive	Imperative
?ana	Hakeet	baHki	?aHki	....
?inta	Hakeet	btiHki	tiHki	?iHki
?inti	Hakeeti	btiHki	tiHki	?iHki
huwwe	Haka	b(y)iHki	yiHki	....
hiyye	Hakat	btiHki	tiHki	....
?iHna	Hakeena	bniHki	niHki	....
?intu	Hakeetu	btiHku	tiHku	?iHku
humme	Haku	b(y)iHku	yiHku	....

Verbs that can be conjugated similarly are:

bada	stanna	sawwa	štara
bana	rama	maša	

The vowel /a/ in the verbs stanna and sawwa does not change in the imperfect form like the rest of the verbs.

Verbs that have past tense pattern similar to those above but different indicative and subjunctive patterns are Habb, Dall, ᶜadd, laff, and Zann.

Pronoun	Past Tense	Present Tense	Subjunctive	Imperative
?ana	Habbeet	baHibb	?aHibb	....
?inta	Habbeet	bitHibb	tHibb	Hibb
?inti	Habbeeti	bitHibbi	tHibbi	Hibbi
huwwe	Habb	biHibb	yHibb	....

hiyye	Habbat	bitHibb	tHibb	....
?iHna	Habbeena	binHibb	nHibb	....
?intu	Habbeetu	bitHibbu	tHibbu	Hibbu
humme	Habbu	biHibbu	yHibbu	....

E. **Exceptional Verbs**

Two exceptional verbs are provided here. These verbs differ from their perspective patterns in one way or another. For example, the imperative for *?aja* is *ta^{c}aal,* which has no phonetic resemblance to *?aja* at all. The glottal stop in*?akal* merges into /a/ in the imperfect, causing /a/ to become /aa/and /?/ to be dropped completely. In the meantime, the first syllable is dropped in the imperative.

1. **?aja/byiiji**

Pronoun	Past Tense	Present Tense	Subjunctive	Imperative
?ana	jiit	baaji	?aaji	....
?inta	jiit	btiiji	tiiji	ta^{c}aal
?inti	jiiti	btiiji	tiiji	ta^{c}aali
huwwe	?aja	b(y)iiji	yiiji	....
hiyye	?ajat	btiiji	tiiji	....
?iHna	jiina	bniiji	niiji	....
?intu	jiitu	btiiju	tiiju	ta^{c}aalu
humme	?aju	b(y)iiju	yiiju	....

2. **?akal/byaakul**

Pronoun	Past Tense	Present Tense	Subjunctive	Imperative
?ana	?akalt	baakul	?aakul	....
?inta	?akalt	btaakul	taakul	kul
?inti	?akalti	btaakli	taakli	kuli
huwwe	?akal	byaakul	yaakul	....
hiyye	?aklat	btaakul	taakul	....
?iHna	?akalna	bnaakul	naakul	....
?intu	?akaltu	btaaklu	taaklu	kulu
humme	?akalu	byaaklu	yaaklu	....

The verb ?axad patterns with ?akal.

Appendix B

Vocabulary Covered in the Course

-Abbreviations used in this appendix;
el. for elative; pl. for plural.

-All verbs are given in the third person singular past tense form, the standard form as used by Arab grammarians and Arabists to designate a verb, followed in brackets by the first singular indicative imperfect form, the form that has been used to introduce verbs in this course.

-Vocabulary in this index are listed according to the following alphabetical order:
?, aa, a, b, ^{c}, D, d, f, ee, g, γ, š, H, h,i, ii, j, k, l, m, n, θ, q, oo, r, S, s, T, t, u, uu, w, x, y, Z, z.

-The symbol / has been used to indicate an alternative pronunciation. It may designate a sound or a word. Semicolon separates two meanings for the same word. The brackets () are used to indicate that the bracketed sound is optional in that word; that is, it can be pronounced or deleted. When used with verbs, it provides the first person singular form.

/?/

?aab	August
?aa^{c}	bottom
?aa^{c}id	sitting, awake
?aam (ba?uum)	to get up
?aasif/mit?assif	sorry
?aasya	Asia
?aazaar/?aaðaar	March
?abadan	not at all
?abil	before
?abil lmiilaad	before Christ (i.e., B.C.)
?abu	father
?abyaD	white
?a^{c}ad (ba^{cc}ud)	to stay, to sit down
?adab	literature
?adar l?imkaan	as much as possible
?adawaat manziliyya	kitchen utensils
?addeeš	how much, long, many
?addeeš btu?mur ?	how much do you order (charge)?
?adiim (el. ?a?dam)	old
?aflaam muγaamaraat	adventure movies
?aHHa (sa^{c}al)	cough
?aHmad	Arabic male name
?aHmar	red
?aHyaanan	sometimes
?ahammiyya	importance
?ahil	family members (especially members of the extended family)
?ahlan wasahlan	welcome
?ahleen	a response to marHaba meaning "hello"
?ahwe	coffee
?ahwe saada	black coffee with no sugar
?aja (baaji)	to come
?ajjar (ba?ajjir)	to rent (your house to someone)
?alaa (ba?li)	to fry

?akal (baakul)	to eat
?alam	a pen, a pencil
?alam (pl. ?aalaam)	pain. The words waja^{c} or mawjuu^{c} are also used to refer to pain in this dialect.
?akil	food
?akil ^{c}arabi	Arabic food
?akla/e	dish, meal
?aliil (el. ?a?al)	a little (less than)
?alla ybaarik fiik	response to mabruuk
?alla ysallmak	God be with you (a response to good-bye)
?allah yin^{c}am ^{c}aleek	a response to na^{c}iiman
?almaani	German
?amar (ba?mur)	to order
?ameerka	the United States
?amraaD jinsiyya	sexually transmitted diseases
?amiiS	a shirt
?ana	I
?aθar (?aaθaar)	ruins
?aθiina	Athens
?ara (ba?ra)	to read
?arba^{c} a	four
?ariib (el. ?a?rab)	close (closer than)
?armani	Armenian
?aSfar	yellow
?aSiir (el. ?a?Sar)	short
?asiir (pl. ?asraa)	war captive
?assalaamu ^{c}alaykum	peace be upon you
?aswad	black
?aTa^{c} (ba?Ta^{c})	to cut off, to cross (a street)
?atraak	Turks
?awi (el. ?a?wa)	strong
?axbaar	news
?axDar	green
?axu (pl. ?axwa)	brother
?ayluul	September
?aywa	yes, yea
?ayy	which
?ayy xidma ya ?ax ?	Can I help you? What can I do for you?
?ayyaar	May
?azra?	blue
?eemta	when
?i?maaš	cloth
?ibil (ba?bal)	to accept
?ibin (pl. wlaad)	son
?ibin ^{c}amm	male cousin from father's side
?ibin xaal	male cousin from mother's side
?i^{c}tamad (ba^{c}tmid)	to be based
?idaarit ?a^{c}maal	business administration
?iddammar	to be destroyed
?idir (ba?dar)	can, to be able to
?ifriiqya	Africa
?iHna	we
?iHtaaj (baHtaaj)	to need
?iima/e	value, price in this context

?iiTaalya	Italy
?ili	I have
?illa	to, before (in describing time), except for
?illi biddak ?iyyaa	whatever you want
?iltihaab	infection
?imm	mother
?imma	either
?imsaak	constipation
?imtiHaan (pl. ?imtiHaanaat)	exam
?in?aTa^c	was/were cut off
?ingliizi	English
?inHara?	to get burnt
?innu	that (a relative word)
?inta	you (masc. sing.)
?inti	you (femin. sing.)
?intifaax	swelling
?intu	you all
?iqtiSaad	economy
?irš	piaster
?isbaani	Spanish
?ishaal	diarrhea
qisim	part, portion
?ism	name
?ista?jar (basta?jir)	to rent
?ista?jar (basta?jir)	to rent (a house for yourself)
?ista^{c}mal (basta^{c}mil)	to use
?istahlak (ba?astahlik)	to consume
?istama^c (ba?astami^c)	to listen
?itaSal (bataSil)	to contact
?itneen	two, Monday
?ittalaata	Tuesday
?ixtaar (baxtaar)	to choose
?ixtalaf (baxtlif)	to differ
?iyyaak	you (objective case)
?iza	if
?iznak ma^{c}ak	a response to ^{c}an ?iznak meaning "with your permission"
?ooγanda	Uganda
?ooroobba	Europe
?uddaam	in front of
?uγniya (pl. ?aγaani)	a song
?ujra	charge, wage
?umma (pl. ?umam)	a nation
?uSSa (pl. ?uSaS)	a story
?usbuu^c	a week
?ustaaz	a professor, teacher
?usturaalya	Australia
?uTT	a cat
?uuma	Indian proper name
?uxt	sister

/b/

ba?aala (pl. ba?aalaat)	a grocery
ba?doonis	parsley

baa?i	the rest
baab	a door
baaba γannuuj (mtabbal)	a Lebanese dish
baa^c (babii^c)	to sell
baarid	cold
baariis	Paris
baaS (pl. baaSaat0	a bus
baasim	Arabic male name
baaxira (pl. bawaaxir)	ship
baayi^c /bayyaa^c (pl. baya^{c}iin)	a salesman
ba^{c}at (bab^{c}at)	to send
ba^{c}D	some
ba^{c}deen	then
ba^{c}id	after
ba^{c}rafš	I don't know
bada (babdi)	to start
badla/e	suit
badla rijaalyiyya	man's suit
badla sitaatiyya	woman's suit
badla walaadiyya	child's suit
badlit sbaaHa	swimming suit
badri	early
baγdaad	Baghdad
baγšiiš	tipping
bakalooryos	bacheolar of arts/science
balad (pl. blaad)	a country
balad (pl. blaad)	a town
baljiika	Belgium
balkoona	balcony
banaa (babni)	to build, to construct
banduura /bandoora	tomatoes
banTaloon	pants
baqqaala (pl. baqqaalaat)	grocery store
bard	stomach flu
bariid baHri	sea mail
bariid ^{c}aadi	regular mail, local mail
bariid jawwi	airmail
bariid msajjal	registered mail
bariiza	a dime
basiiT	simple, small
baskaleet	a bicycle
bass	only
baTaaTa	potatoes
baTii?	slow
baToon	concrete
baTTiix	watermelon
bazeella	peas
b^{c}iid ^{c}an	far from
bee^c	sale
beeD	eggs
been	between
been quseen/?useen	between brackets
beet	a house

beet laHim	Bethlehem
beetinjaan	eggplants
beruut	Beirut
bhaar (bhaaraat)	a spice
bidaaya	beginning
bidd	to want
biduun	without
biššifaa? nšaalla	I wish you recovery
biši^{c}	ugly
biira	beer
bil?iDaafa ?ilaa	in addition to
binni	brown
bint (pl. banaat)	a girl, a daughter
bint ^{c}amm	a female cousin from father's side
bint xaal	a female cousin from mother's side
birka	a pool
birkit sbaaHa	a swimming pool
bitta?siiT	through financing
bitwa??af ^{c}ala	it depends on
biZZabT	exactly
blaatiin	platinum
blaaš	free
bluuza	a blouse
bnaaya (pl. binaayaat)	a building
boot	a sport shoe
bsur^{c}a	at a speed of
bukra	tomorrow
burj	tower
burt?aana (pl. burt?aan)	an orange
burt?aani	orange (a color)
burtuɣaali	Portuguese
bxaaTrak	good-bye
bxeer	good

/^{c}/

^{c}aadatan	usually
^{c}aadil	Arabic male name
^{c}aalaj (ba^{c}aalij)	to treat
^{c}aalam	the world
^{c}aali (el. ?a^{c}la)	high
^{c}aamal (ba^{c}aamil)	to deal with
^{c}aamil (pl. ^{c}ummaal)	a worker
^{c}aaSif	stormy
^{c}aayiz	I need
^{c}abba (ba^{c}abbi)	to fill out
^{c}abba (ba^{c}abbi)	to fill in
^{c}abiir	Arabic female's name
^{c}abr (l^{c}uSuur)	through
^{c}aDim (pl. ^{c}Daam)	a bone
^{c}adad	number
^{c}adnaan	Arabic male name

^{c}afš beet	furniture
^{c}afwan	a response to šukran meaning "you are welcome"
^{c}ašaan	in order to
^{c}ašaanak/ik	for yourself, because of you
^{c}ašara	ten
^{c}ala (prep.)	a preposition that takes several meanings such as on, to, above
^{c}ala ?ayyit Haal	however
^{c}ala ?eeš	on what?
^{c}ala bu^{c}ud	at a distance
^{c}ala l?a?al/?aliila	at least
^{c}ala l?aktar	at the most
^{c}ala Tuul	right away
^{c}amal	making
^{c}amm	an uncle (father's brother)
^{c}ammaan	Amman
^{c}an/ba^{c}d ?iznak	idioms that indicate the intention of departing
^{c}arabi	Arabic, an Arab
^{c}ariiD (el. ?a^{c}raD)	wide
^{c}ariiq (el. ?a^{c}raq)	ancient
^{c}aSiir-burt?aan	orange juice
^{c}aZiim	great
^{c}azzaabi	single (unmarried)
^{c}eela (pl. ^{c}yal, ^{c}elaat)	a family
^{c}ibaara (pl. ^{c}ibaaraat)	utterance
^{c}idda/e	several
^{c}iid miilaad	Christmas
^{c}ilaaj	treatment
^{c}ilm lkumbyuutar	computer science
^{c}imaara	building
^{c}imil (ba^{c}mal)	to do
^{c}inab	grapes
^{c}iyaada	clinic
^{c}uluum ^{c}askariyya	military sciences
^{c}umur	age
^{c}umuula	charge, commission
^{c}uTla/e	break, holiday

/D/

Daa^{c} (baDii^{c})	to get lost
Daaf (badiif)	to add
DaaHiya (pl. DawaaHi)	suburb
Dall (baDall)	to stay; to continue
Daxm	huge
Dayyi? (el. ?aDya?)	narrow
DDuhur	noon

/d/

d?ii?a (pl. da?aayi?)	a minute
daa?ira (pl. dawaayit)	department
daafi (el. ?adfa)	warm
daaxil	inside
daayman	always; an expression used to thank someone for a meal
dafa^c (badfa^c)	to pay
daftar	a notebook
dahab	gold
dahuud	David
daktoor	doctor
daraja (pl. darajaat)	class; step; degree
daraja ?uula	first class
daraja taanya	economy class
darraaja	a motorcycle
dawa (pl. ?adwiya)	medicine
dawli	international
dawwar (badawwir)	to look for
daxal (badxul)	to get into
daxlik	an inceptive marker used to initiate an inquiry or a request
daxxan (badaxxin)	to smoke
di??a	accuracy
diin (pl. diyaanaat/?adyaan)	religion
diinaar (pl. danaaniir)	dinar
dili^c	plain
dimašq	Damascus
diraasa (pl. diraasaat)	study
dirham	a monetary unit used in some parts of the Arab world
dooxa	dizziness
duγri	straight
duktooraa	doctorate
durraa?	beaches

/f/

faaDi	empty; free
faatiH	light (for colors)
faaTma/e	Arabic female name
faatuura (pl. fawaatiir)	a bill
faayda	use
faHaS (bafHaS)	to check
fahmaan	knowledgeable
fakk (bafukk)	to break (a dollar into change)
fakka/e	change
fakkar (bafakkir)	to think
falaafil	a type of Arabic food that consists of hummus fried balls
falawanza/fluwanza	flu
falsafa/e	philosophy
fan (pl. fnuun)	art
far? (pl. furuu?)	difference
faram (bafrum)	to cut into pieces, to chop
faransa	France
faransi	French
faSuuliya	beans

fataH (baftaH)	to open
fawaakih/faakha	fruit
fawzi	Arabic proper name
faxim	magnificent
fi (prep.)	a preposition that has several meanings based on the context
fi/bi l?afraaH ?inšaalla	an expression used to show gratitude for being provided with a meal or drink
fi l?axiir	at last
fi^{c}il (?af^{c}aal)	verb
fi^{c}lan	real
fiDDa	silver
fiš ?ayy maani^c	there is no objection
fihim (bafham)	to understand
fiizya	physics
filfil	pepper
filisTiin	Palestine
film (pl. ?aflaam)	a movie
fils (pl. fluus)	one-tenth of an ?irš (equivalent to one cent)
foo?	on top of
fundu? (pl. fanaadi?)	hotel
furn (pl. fruun)	a stove
fusTaan (pl. fasaTiin)	a dress
fuul	fava beans

/g/ and /γ/

garaaj (pl. garaajaat)	a garage
γaali (el. ?aγla)	expensive
γaami?	dark (for colors)
γaayim	cloudy
γaaz	burner
γabi (el. ?aγba)	stupid
γarb	west
γariib	strange
γasal (baγsul)	to wash
γurfa (pl. γuraf)	a room
γurfit juluus	living room
γurfit noom	bedroom
γurfit Sufra	dining room

/š/

ša?fa/e (pl. šu?af)	a piece
šaari^c (pl. sawaari^c)	a street
ša(a)wirma	a Middle Eastern dish
šaay	tea
ša^{c}b (pl. šu^{c}uub)	people
šadda/e	cards
šahaadit milaad	birth certificate
šahar (pl. shuur)	a month
šakil	shape
šamaal	north
šamaal γarb	northwest
šamaal šar?	northeast

šams	sun
šanta (pl. šunat)	a bag
šar?	east
šaTranj	chess
šaTT lbaHar	beach
šbaaT	February
ši (pl. ?ašyaa?)	a thing
šibšib; babuuj	slippers
ši^{c}ir	poetry
šifaa?	recovery
šiiškabaab	a Middle Eastern dish
šilin	a five-piaster coin
šimmaam	melon
širib (bašrab)	to drink
šita	winter
šriik (pl. šuraka)	a partner
šooka (pl. šwak)	a fork
štaɣal (baštɣil)	to work
šu	what
šu l?uSSa ?	What's the matter?
šu maalak ?	What's the matter ?
šubbaak (pl. šabaabiik)	a window
šufeer; sawwaa? (pl. šufariyya)	a driver
šukran	thank you
šwayy	a little

/H/

Haa?iT lmabkaa	the Wailing Wall
Haadis sayyaara	car accident
Haarr	hot; spicy
Haawal (baHaawil)	to try
Habb (baHibb)	to like, to love
Habba/e (pl. Habbaat)	pill, tablet
HaDar (baHDur)	to attend
HaDDar (baHaDDir)	to prepare
Had/a (?aHad/waaHad)	someone
Hadii?a; jneena (pl. Hadaayi?)	yard (garden)
Hafar (baHfur)	to dig
Hajar	stone
Hajaz (baHjiz)	to reserve
Hajm (pl. Hjaam)	size
Hajz	reservation
Haka (baHki)	to speak, to talk
Hakiim (el. ?aHkam)	wise
Hilawiyaat	sweets
Haliib	milk
Hamaawa	fever
Hamal (baHmil)	to carry; to hold
Hammaam (pl. Hammaamaat)	bathroom
Hanaan	Arabic female name
Hara? (baHri?)	to burn
Harb lxaliij	the Gulf War
Harkat sseer	traffic
Harrak (baHarrik)	to stir

Hasaasiyya	allergy
Hasab (baHsub)	to count, to calculate
Hasan	Arabic male name
HaTT (baHuTT)	to deposit; to place; to put
Hatta	until
Hawl	around
Hawwal (baHawwil)	to transfer
Hayy	alive
Hayy (pl. ?aHyaa?)	a quarter
Hda^{c}š	eleven
HeeT (pl. HeeTaan)	wall
Hilu (el. ?aHla)	nice; sweet
Hiwaar (pl. Hiwaaraat)	a dialogue
Hsaab (pl. Hsaabaat)	account
Hsaab jaari	checking account
Hsaab tawfiir	saving account
HummuS	chickpeas
Hurr	free
Huzayraan	June
Hzaam; ?i?šaaT	a belt

/h/

haada	this (masc.)
haadi	this (femin.)
haadi (?ahda)	quiet
haala	Arabic female name
hadaak	that (masc.)
hadiik	that (femin.)
hadool	these (femin. and masc.)
halla(?)	now
handasa	engineering
haram (pl. ?ahraam)	a pyramid
hawiyya	identity card
hayy	abbreviation for haada or haadi
hiyye	she
hoon	here
humme	they
hunaak	there
huwwe	he

/j/

jaaff	dry
jaahiz	ready
jaaj	chicken
jaam^{c}a (pl. jaam^{c}aat)	a university
jaar (pl. jiraan)	neighbor
jaawab (bajaawib)	to answer, to respond
jaay	coming
jadd; siid	grandfather
jadda; sitt	grandmother
jaγraafya	geography
jakeet	jacket
jalas (bajlis)	to sit down

jamaal	beauty
jam^{c}an	a response to mwaffa?
jamii^{c}	all of
jamiil	Arabic male name
janaaH (?ajniHa)	a suite in a hotel
janb	next to; close
januub	south
januub γarb	southwest
januub šar?	southeast
jariida (pl. jaraayid)	newspaper
jarrab (bajarrib)	to try
jawaaz safar	passport
jawla (pl. jawlaat)	a tour
jayyidan	carefully
jaziira (pl. jazaa?ir)	an island
jdiid (el. ?ajdad)	new
jneeh (pl. jneehaat)	pound
joo^{c}aan	hungry
jubne/jibne	cheese
jurH (pl. jruuH)	a wound
juz?iyyan	partially
juzdaan	wallet

/k/

kaan (bakuun)	to be
kaanuun ?awwal	December
kaanuun taani	January
kaasa/e (pl. kaasaat)	a glass
kaaš	cash
kabbuut (pl. kabaabiit)	a coat
kabsa	the national Saudi dish
kafitiirya	cafeteria
kahraba	electricity
kakaaw	cocoa
kalb (pl. klaab)	a dog
kam	how many or how much
kamaal	Arabic male name
kamara (pl. kamaraat)	camera
kammal (bakammil)	to continue
kammuun	cumin
karaz	cherry
kart viisa	Visa card
kaslaan	lazy
kasir (pl. ksuur)	a fracture
katab (baktub)	to write
kazzaab	liar
kbiir (el. ?akbar)	big
kibir (bakbar)	to grow
kifaaya	enough
kiif	how
kiif Haalak	How are you? (masc. sing.)
kiif Haalik	How are you? (femin. sing.)
kiif-i-lHaal	How are you? (generic)
kiimya	chemistry

kilma/e (pl. kilmaat)	a word
kniisit li?yaama	Church of the Holy Sepulchre
kniisit lmahid	Church of the Nativity in Bethlehem
koola	any soda product
ktaab (pl. kutub)	a book
kufta/kifte	an Arab dish made of ground meat, onion, parsley, etc.
kuHuul; mašruub	alcohol
kull ^{c}aam winta bxeer	an expression that can be roughly equated with "happy new year." Its literal meaning "happy anniversary" or " many happy returns."
kull yoom	every day
kulna ... ma ^{c}ada	all of us except
kumiidi	comedian
kundara (pl. kanaadir)	dress shoe
kurat lqadam	soccer
kurat lyad	hand ball
kurat rriiša	badminton
kurat ssalla	basketball
kurat TTaa?ira	volleyball
kursi (pl. karaasi)	a chair
kuskus; maftuul	Moroccan national dish
kuurya/kuuriyya	Korea
kwayyis	good, well

/l/

l?aHad	Sunday
l?amir lilaah/la ?allah	a compliment meaning literally "order be to God!"
l?arb^{c}a	Wednesday
l?injiil	Gospels
l?uds	Jerusalem
l?umam lmutaHida	the United Nations
l?urdun	Jordan
la ... wala	neither ... nor
la?	no
laa zaal	still
laazim	must
laban	yogurt
laHim	meat
laHimit ^{c}ijil	beef
laHimit xanziir	pork
laHimit xaruuf	lamb
laHZa	a moment
laHZa, min faDlak	a moment, please!
lamma	when (a relative word)
lamuun	lemon
lbank lmarkazi	central bank
lbaraaziil	Brazil
l^{c}iraaq	Iraq
leela (pl. layaali)	a night
leera (pl. leeraat)	a monetary unit used in Lebanon and Syria
li^{c}ib (bal^{c}ab)	to play
mašγuul	busy
mašhuur	popular, famous
maši	walking

lHa?ii?a	the truth, in fact
lHamdilla	a response to kiif lHaal meaning "thanks be to God"
lhind	India
li?annu	because
libis (balbis)	to put clothes on
liibya	Libya
likuweet	Kuwait
liθθa	teeth gum
liSS (pl. luSuuS)	a thief
li/awaHdi	alone
ljaay	coming
ljary; rrakD	running, jogging
ljaww	weather
ljazaa?ir	Algeria
ljum^{c}a	Friday
llid	Lod
lmaɣrib	Morocco
lmaksiik	Mexico
lmasjid l?aqSa	the Aqsa Mosque
looH (pl. lwaaH)	blackboard
loon (pl. ?alwaan)	a color
lqaahira	Cairo
lqur?aan	Qur'an
lubnaan	Lebanon
lu^{c}ba/e (pl. ?al^{c}aab)	a game
luɣa (pl. luɣaat)	a language
lxamiis	Thursday
lyaabaan	Japan
lyaanaSiib	lottery
lyaman	Yemen

/m/

m?addas	holy
ma ti?la?š	don't worry!
ma?li	fried
ma?luube	Palestinian national dish
ma?suum	divided
maaDi	last
maahir	Arabic male name
maani^c	objection
maaTir; mšatti	rainy
mablaɣ	amount (of money)
mabni	built, constructed
mabruuk	congratulations
ma^c (prep.)	with
ma^c miin	with who/whom
ma^c zaalik	though, despite that
ma^c-i-ssalaama	good-bye
ma^{c}diyya	ferry
ma^{c}karoona	macaroni
ma^{c}luumaat	information

ma^{c}naa (pl. ma^{c}aani)	meaning
ma^{c}naaha	in that case
ma^{c}ruuD	displayed (for)
ma^{c}ruuD lalbee^c	for sale
madhuun	rubbed with, painted
madiina (pl. mudun)	a city
madxal (pl. madaaxil)	entrance
maftuuH	open
maHal malaabis	clothing store
maHal tijaari	store
maHalli	local
maHaTTit baaSaat	bus station
maHsuub	included
majalla (pl. majallaat)	a magazine
majisteer	master's (degree)
majnuun	crazy
makaan (?amaakin)	a place
maktab (pl. makaatib)	an office
maktab (pl. makaatib)	a desk
maktab lbariid; poosta	post office
maktaba (pl. maktabaat)	bookstore; library
maktuub (pl. makatiib)	a letter
malaabis	clothes
mal^{c}ab (pl. malaa^{c}ib)	a playground
maliiš	I do not have
malyaan	full
malyoon	a million
mamar (pl. mamarraat)	aisle
mamnuu^c	forbidden
mansaf	Jordanian national dish
manTiqa	area
marbaH	interest
mara?a	broth
maraD (pl. ?amraaD)	disease
marawaana; Hašiiš	marijuana
marHaba	hello
mariiD; ^{c}ayyaan (pl. marDa)	patient
markaz (pl. maraakiz)	a center
marr (bamurr)	to stop by
marra (pl. marraat)	once
marraat	sometimes
marwaan	Arabic male name
maSir	Egypt
maSna^c (pl. maSaani^c)	a factory
mas?uuf	roofed
masa lxeer	good evening!
masa nnuur	a response to masa lxeer meaning "good evening"
masaaHa	area
masak (bamsik)	to catch
masiiHi	a Christian
maskiin	poor, pathetic, lost
masluu?	boiled
masmuuH	allowed
masraH (pl. masaariH)	a theater

masraHiyya (pl. masraHiyyaat)	a play
massal (bamassil)	to represent
maTaar (pl. maTaaraat)	an airport
maTbax (pl. maTaabix)	kitchen
maT^{c}am (pl. maTaa^{c}im)	a restaurant
mawjuud	available, exists
mawqi^{c} (pl. mawaaqi^{c})	location
maxraj (pl. maxaarij)	an exit
mayy/e	water
mazbuuT	right
mbaariH	yesterday
mHaasib (pl. mHaasbiin)	teller
mHammar	roasted
mhandis (pl. mhandsiin)	engineer
mi/a^{c}la?a (pl. ma^{c}aali?)	a spoon
miš baTTaal	not bad
miš muhim	It does not matter.
miš	not
mišmiš	apricot
miil (pl. ?amyaal)	a mile
miin	who
milH	salt
min (prep.)	from
min ?abil	before
min ?eeš	of what?
min faDlak	please
min marra	not at all
min ween	from where?
mitil	like, such as
mitir (pl. mtaar)	meter
mitzawwij/mitjawwiz	married
mjawharaat, siiγa	jewelry
mka^{cc}ab	cubic
mlawan	color
mluxiyya	Jewish mallow (a form of plant)
mnaasib	convenient
mneen	short form of min ween
mniiH	good, well
mooz	bananas
mrabba^{c}	square
msaafir (pl. msaafriin)	a traveler
msajjal	registered
msakkar	closed
mu?tamar	a conference
mubaašir	direct
mu^{c}tadil	moderate
mu^{c}Zam	most
mudda/e	period
muftaaH	open
muHaami	lawyer
muHaasaba/e	accounting
muHtawayaat	contents, ingredients
mujrim	criminal
mukaalama tilifooniyya	a telephone call

mumkin	Is it possible?
muna	female Arabic name
munaasaba (pl. munaasabaat)	occasion
muntazah (pl. muntazahaat)	a park
muriiH	comfortable
musalsal (pl. musalsalaat)	television show
musbaqan	in advance
musiiqa l^{c}arabiyya	Arabic music
musta^{c}id (pl. musta^{c}iddiin)	ready
mut^{c}ib	tiresome
mutlij/mtallij	snowy
mušmis	sunny
mwaffa?	good luck!
mwaZZaf (pl. mwaZZafiin)	employee

/n/

na?a^{c} (ban?a^{c})	to soak
naam (banaam)	to sleep
naar	fire
naaTiHaat ssaHaab	skyscrapers
naayim	sleeping
nabi	prophet
na^{c}am	yes
na^{c}iiman	a polite expression used to acknowledge noticing that someone has shaved, taken a shower, has had a hair cut, etc.
naDDaaraat	glasses
nafs	same, self
našiiT	active
naSaH (banSaH)	to recommend, to advise
nasama	person
nbasaT (baninsiT)	to enjoy oneself, to have a good time
neers (pl. neersaat)	a nurse
nšaalla	God willing!
niisaan	April
nisi (bansa)	to forget
niZaam	system
nizil (banzil)	to land; to register at a hotel; to step down,
njaaS	pears
nnamsa	Austria
nnarwiij	Norway
nuSS	half
nyuuzilanda	New Zealand

/q/

qaamuus (pl. qawaamiis)	a dictionary
qaanuun	law
qarya (pl. quraa)	a village
qiTaar	train
qiT^{c}a (pl. qiTa^{c})	a paragraph
qubbat SSaxra	Dome of the Rock

/r/

r?ii? (el. ?ara?)	thin
ra?S	dancing
ra?san	right away
raadyo (pl. radyuwaat)	radio
raaH (baruuH)	to go
raas baSal	an onion head
raay	opinion
raayiH	going
rabii^{c}	spring
rabTa; graafa	a tie
raDDa/e	a bruise
radd (barudd)	to answer
rajja^{c} (barajji^{c})	to send, put, take back
rakaD (barkuD)	to jog
ramaadi; sakani	gray
raqam	number
ramil	sand
ramli	sandy
rana	Arabic female name
rann (i.e., rann ttalafoon)	to ring
raTib/riTib	humid
rašiH	cold
rašiid	Arabic female name
rγiif (pl. ruγfaan, turuufa)	a loaf of bread
ribiH (barbaH)	to win
riHla (pl. riHlaat)	a trip
riHla mwaffa?a	have a nice trip!
riim	Arabic female name
riji^{c} min (barja^{c} min)	to return
risaala (pl. rasaayil)	a letter
riyaaD	Arabic male name
riyaaDiyyaat	mathematics
roomansi	romantic
rriyaaD	Riyadh
riyaaDa	sport
rubu^{c}	quarter, one-fourth
rušeeta	prescription
rukba/e	knee
ruusi	Russian
ruzz	rice
rxiiS	cheap

/S/

Saala	salon (a hall in a hotel)
Saar (baSiir)	to become; to have been; to start
SabaaH-i-lxeer	good morning
SabaaH-i-nnuur	a response to good morning
Sadii? (sadaayi?)	a friend
Saff (pl. Sfuuf)	a class
SaHiiH	correct
SaHin (pl. SHuun)	a plate

SaHteen	a response to daayman or fi l?afraaH nšaalla! meaning " I wish you a double health."
SaHteen w^{c}aafya	a response to daayman or fi l?afraaH nšaalla! meaning "I wish you a double health and health."
Saraf (baSruf)	to cash, to spend
SaraTa/SalaTa	salad
Saydaliyya	pharmacy
Seef	summer
Siiγa (pl. Siyaγ)	a form of a verb
Sinaa^{c}a	industry
Sinf (pl. ?aSnaaf)	type
Siraa^c	conflict
SSiin	China
SubuH	morning
Suddaa^c; waja^c raaS	headache
Sufra daayma	an expression of gratitude used to express appreciation for a meal
Suur	a wall
Suura (pl. Suwar)	a picture

/s/

sa?al (bas?al)	to ask
saa? (basuu?)	to drive
saadwiš, saandwiiša	sandwich
saafar ^{c}ala (basaafir ^{c}ala)	to travel
saaHil (pl. sawaaHil)	shore
saamiya	Arabic female name
saayiH/a (pl. suyyaaH)	tourist
sabaanix/γ	spinach
sabab	reason, cause
sabaH (basbaH)	to swim
sab^{c}a	seven
safra (pl. safraat)	trip
saHab (basHab)	to withdraw
sakan (baskun)	to live
sakkar (basakkir)	to close
sala? (baslu?)	to boil
salaam	peace
salaamtak	nothing but your comfort and safety
salafan	in advance
saliim	Arabic male name
salla/e (pl. sallaat)	basket
sallim ^{c}ala	say hello to, send my regards to
salwa	Arabic female name
samaH (basmaH)	to permit
samaka (pl. samak, samakaat)	a fish
sammuuna (pl. sammuunaat)	telephone token
sana (pl. sniin)	a year
sarii^c	fast
sawsan	Arabic female name
sayyaara (pl. sayyaaraat)	a car
sayyid (pl. saada)	mister, sir
sbaaHa	swimming
see^{c}a (pl. see^{c}aat)	time; watch; clock; an hour

sɣiir (el. ?azɣar)	small, little
si^{c}ir (pl. ?as^{c}aar)	price
sihil (pl. ?ashal)	easy
siid	grandfather
si(i)gaara	cigarette
siirial; koorn fleeks	cereal
sikirteer/a	secretary
sikkiina (pl. sakaakiin)	a knife
simi^c (basma^c)	to hear, to listen
si/ummaak	sumac (a spicey herb)
sinama	cinema, theater
sitta	six
sitt (pl. sittaat)	a lady
siyaaHa	tourism
siyaasa	politics
siyaasi	tactful
ssa/u^{c}uudiyya	Saudi Arabia
ssbaaHa	swimming
ssabt	Saturday
suu?	market
suuši	a Japanese dish
ssuudaan	Sudan
ssuweed	Sweden
stanna (bastanna)	to wait
stariiH (bastriiH); trayyaH	be seated, have a seat
sukkaan	dwellers, population
sukkar	sugar
suuriyya	Syria
swiisra	Switzerland

/T/

Ta?iyya (pl. Tawaa?i)	a hat
Taab (baTiib)	to recover
Taabi? (pl. Tawaabi?)	floor
Taabi^c (pl. Tawaabi^c)	stamp
Taalib (pl. Tullaab)	a student
Taali^c	rising
Taawla (pl. Taawlaat)	a table
Taaza	fresh
Taba?a (pl. Taba?aat)	a layer
Taba^c (baTba^c)	to type
Tab^{c}an	of course
Tabax (baTbux)	to cook
Tabii^{c}a	nature
Tabiix	cooked food
Ta^{c}im	taste
TaHan (baTHan)	to grind
Talab (pl. Talabaat)	application
Tamir; ^{c}ajwa	dates (a fruit)
Tard (pl. Truud)	package, parcel
Tari	soft, tender
Tarii? (pl. Turu?)	way, road

Tawiil (el. ?aTwal)	long; tall
Tawwal (baTawwil)	to take long time
THiina	sesame butter
Tib	medicine
Tili^{c} (baTla^{c})	to become; to rise; to take off
Tna^{c}š	twelve
TTa?s	weather
Tunjara (pl. Tanaajir)	cooking pot

/ t /

t?axxar (bat?axxar)	to be late
ta?miin	insurance
ta?riiban	approximately
taali	following
taani	second; other
taariix	history; date
tabbuule	a Lebanese dish
ta^{c}baan	tired
ta^{c}liim	education
tadfi?a	heating
tašriin ?awwal	October
tašriin taani	November
taHt (prep.)	under
tajwiif; xuzu? (pl. tajaawiif)	a cavity
taklifa (pl. takaaliif)	cost, expense
takyiif (hawaa?i)	air-conditioning
talaata	three
talafoon (pl. talafoonaat)	a telephone
talafoon ^{c}umuumi	public phone
tamaanya	eight
taman	price, value
tammuuz	July
tamtaaz	to be distinguished
tannuura (pl. tanaaniir)	a skirt
taqa^{c}	to lie, to be situated
tarak (batruk)	to leave
tarbiya	education
taxt mifrid	twin bed
taxt mijwiz	double bed
tazkara (pl. tazaakir)	a ticket
tazkara raayiH bass	one-way ticket
tazki/ara raayiH-jaay	two-way ticket
t^{c}allam (bat^{c}allam)	to learn
t^{c}arraf ^{c}ala (bat^{c}arraf)	to meet, to get introduced to
tfaDDal	here you are!
tfarraj ^{c}ala (batfarraj ^{c}ala)	to watch
tšammas (batšammas)	to sun bathe
tšarrafna	nice to meet you!
tHassan (batHassan)	to improve
tiin	figs
tijaara	trade
ti/alivisyoon (pl. tilvizyoonaat)	a television
timsaal lHuriyya	Statue of Liberty

tinis	table tennis
tinis ?arDi	tennis
tis^{c}a	nine
tiStbiH ^{c}ala xeer	good night!
tjawwal (batjawwal)	to wander
tkallam (batkallam)	to speak
tkawwan	to be made of
tna??al (batna??al)	to move around
tneen	two
tu?umr	at your service!
tuffaaHa (pl. tuffaaH)	an apple
tult	one-third
turkiyya	Turkey
tuunis	Tunis
twakkal ^{c}ala llaa	go on, proceed (rely on God)!
tzawwaj/tjawwaz (batzawwaj)	to get married

/w/

w-	and; while
wa??a^{c} (bawa??i^{c})	to sign
wa??af (bawa??if)	to stop
waa?if	stopping; standing up
waa?il	Arabic proper name
waaHad	one
wa^{c}alaykum-i-ssalaam	a respone to ssalaamu ^{c}alaykum meaning "and peace be upon you too"
wajad (balaa?i)	to find (a place closed)
wajbit-i-l^{c}aša	supper; dinner
wajbit lγada	dinner; lunch
wajbit lifTuur	breakfast
wajja^{c} (bawajji^{c})	to hurt, to cause pain
wakiil ssafar	travel agent
wala ši	nothing
wala yhimmak	don't worry!
walaaw	expression of surprise
walad (pl. wlaad)	a boy
waliid	Arabic proper name
waθaa?iqi	documentary
war?at xamis danaaniir	five-dinar bill
wara	behind
wara? ^{c}inab	grape leaves (Middle Eastern dish)
wara?a (pl. wara?)	a sheet, piece of paper
warda	Arabic female name
waSaT	center
waSSaf (bawaSSif)	to describe
ween	where
wi?i^{c} (ba?a^{c})	to fall down
willa	or; of course
winta min ?ahlu	a response to tiStbiH ^{c}ala xeer

/x/

xaal (pl. xwaal)	an uncle (from mother's side)

xaarTa (pl. xawaariT)	a map
xaaSS	special
xabar (pl. ?axbaar)	news
xadiija	Arabic female name
xafiif	light
xalf	back (of the check)
xalla (baxalli)	to keep ; to let
xallaS (baxalliS)	to finish
xallaT (baxalliT)	to mix
xamir; nbiid	wine
xariif	autumn
xaSim	discount
xaTiib	a fiance
xaTiir (el. ?axTar)	dangerous
xaTT	script
xeer	good news, I hope!
xidma (pl. xidmaat)	service
xoox	plums
xubz	bread
xuDra	vegetables
xuSuuSi	private
xyaar	cucumber

/y/

yaasiin	Arabic male name
yabdu	it seems
yabuusiyyiin	Jebusites (the people who founded Jerusalem)
ya^{c}ni	meaning, that is, in other words
ya^{c}ni	kind of
yahuudi	a Jew, Jewish
yamiin	right (as in right hand)
yoom (pl. ?ayyaam)	a day

/Z/

Zann (baZunn)	to think, to believe
Zarf (pl. Zruuf)	an envelop

/z/

zahar	cauliflower
zaki (pl. ?azka)	clever
zamaan	long ago
zamiil (pl. zumalaa?)	partner of some sort
zayy maa biddak	as you wish
zbuun (pl. zabaayin)	customer
zeet	oil
zeet zeetuun	olive oil
zeetuun	olives
zift	bad
ziraa^{c}a	farming, agriculture
zooj/jooz	husband
zooja/jooza	wife
zubda/e	butter